A Good Night Out

Popular Theatre:
Audience, Class and Form

JOHN McGRATH

A Good Night Out

Popular Theatre:
Audience, Class and Form

With a Foreword by
Raymond Williams

METHUEN DRAMA

A METHUEN PAPERBACK

First published in Great Britain in 1981 in simultaneous hard-back and paperback editions by Eyre Methuen Ltd.
Reprinted 1982, 1984 and 1986 by Methuen London Ltd.

Reprinted in 1989 by Methuen Drama,
Michelin House, 81 Fulham Road, London,
SW3 6RB and distributed in the United
States of America by HEB Inc, 70 Court Street,
Portsmouth, New Hampshire 03801.

ISBN 0 413 49330 X (Hardback)
ISBN 0 413 48700 8 (Paperback)

Printed and bound in Great Britain by
Cox & Wyman Ltd, Reading

CONTENTS

FOREWORD

by Raymond Williams

This book contains six talks given by John McGrath to a seminar in Cambridge in 1979. He was in Cambridge as the first Visiting Fellow on the Judith E. Wilson Fund of the Faculty of English. The purpose of this Fund is to encourage contacts between people working in professional drama and literature and those in the university who are studying or intending to go on to them. There had been annual and occasional lectures for some twenty years, but an expansion of the Fund made this more extended kind of visit possible.

We were very lucky to have John McGrath to inaugurate this Fellowship. It can be said that almost any kind of contact between professionals and academics, in this influential area, is useful or is at least better than nothing. But the situation is more complex than that. Cambridge not only has a very active tradition of undergraduate activity in theatre and writing, from which, for many years but especially in the last twenty, an exceptional number of people have gone on to such work professionally; the entry into television and theatre has been remarkable. But also the university has theatricalities of its own, deep in its own processes, and some of these overawe not only the innocent and the unwary but also many experienced professionals.

There is then a rather ridiculous way in which University and Theatre can make contact: University charmingly theatrical; Theatre allusive and by-the-way scholarly. But even if this public-relations encounter is avoided there are other likely kinds of failure. Beyond or behind or at best ignoring its theatricalities, the university is in practice a plain old place, with a good deal of learning but also a good deal of ignorance. When it sets out, in its own best spirit, to remedy an area of ignorance, it wants and certainly needs plain talk and plain information. Yet those seeing only its public projection and its theatrically impressive manners can, when invited to talk to it, adapt altogether too much. 'My God', you can infer or sometimes even hear, 'I am giving a lecture at *Cambridge*'. You can then get people pulling back from what they think, and from what they think about, in some sketch of what is supposed to be an academic manner: be solemn, be balanced, don't talk about yourself.

Yet of course the one thing Cambridge already has in abundance is academic talk, at its best and its worst. In the areas in which it has some crucial kinds of ignorance, the last thing it needs is that kind of adaptation. Thus students and their teachers read plays and novels, watch films and go to the theatre, but at work they almost inevitably take these as made, ready-made, for their study. There is a powerful tendency to see not men and women behind them but merely names (and of course dates). Then it is not only important for some actual man or woman involved in their making to appear. It is crucial that he should talk from his own ground, in his own way, and that he should include his kind of thinking, about how to write and produce and arrange and make his living, rather than suppress all this in the interests of critical consumption or author's tips for critical consumption.

He can in any case be certain that this other kind of thinking will already be present, and that he will have plenty of chances to take part in it, where necessary, once his own view of the process has been established.

The strength of John McGrath's seminar was that from his first words he took up this independent position. He went on to give a great deal of information and a sustained argument of an important and radical point of view. It was very good for Cambridge, as the response showed. It is also good that the talks are now available, in this book, for a much wider group.

Of course the conditions were in some senses right. The term of the seminar was what somebody – with heavy literary breathing – was already calling the Winter of Discontent. I remember being with John McGrath at a meeting in a draughty lecture-room in Trinity, to support the NUPE strikers. The Regional Officer's exposition of the wages of a sewerman had a fine clarity, at once ironic and necessary just off the moonlight of Great Court. It was a kind of communication which connects very clearly with part of what McGrath says about theatre. On another even colder night, the streets glazed with packed snow, he and I got somehow lost together in that new part of King's which some call Alphaville, at a time when I was already due in another part of the college to give a paper on 'The Bloomsbury Fraction'. The connections and the ironies, the tensions and yet the determinations, were especially alive in those weeks: one of those fortunate terms in which even the most difficult intellectual arguments are hard, clear and uncompromising.

Yet still the decisive contribution was McGrath's unique combination of an exceptionally varied experience, in prestigious theatres and in his pioneering roadshows, and in television and cinema, with so active a sense of having learned to some purpose: a purpose which

he at once declares and with unusual spirit argues for and
encourages, against so many prevailing resignations and
cynicisms, to say nothing of more orthodox adjustments.
He is hard on many of his contemporaries, but mainly in
terms of the social and cultural forms to which they have
adapted or which they have come willingly to represent.
What he says, for example, about 1956 and the Royal
Court – that heavily mythicised moment – not only
needed saying but comes with particular appropriateness
from him, since he has at once been close to it and yet
shown the possibility of other plays and other ways. Or
take the different kind of disagreement with Trevor Griffiths, about television drama. I happen to think that this
is still an open question, and we have from time to time
disagreed about it. But what McGrath says – and for that
matter, with his different emphases, what Griffiths says –
has the particular authority of long practice and experi-
ment and reflection, and that makes it quite unlike criticism, in the ordinary consumer sense, or mere factional
disagreement in defence of one's own unique sector.

Still, the main drive of the talks is a contemporary case
for theatre, of a kind which can only happen by deliberate
distancing from what is conventionally established as
Theatre. What interests me about this is its connection
with the quite different work I and some others have been
doing about the 'audience' – in that significant way of
describing it – and its active or passive role in the actual
creation of dramatic forms. I have worked on this in
history and theory (and incidentally would add that the
history of the nineteenth-century theatre, including melodrama, would significantly extend McGrath's case).
John McGrath has not only observed this; he has gone out
and tested the possibility of new forms for new
'audiences' – new groupings of people, and especially
British working-class people, in what are necessarily

altered relationships to writers and actors and, where it works, to each other.

His importance in contemporary British culture is that he has followed this road with a seriousness, a professional skill and a resilience that are, in this necessary combination, outstanding. His term in Cambridge was an opportunity for reflection and argument, and for telling others about what he was doing and meaning to do. That is the best sense of contact between university and profession. That is why these lively and considered talks are so well worth listening to and now reading.

PREFACE

The following pieces bear all the marks of what they were: a series of weekly talks to undergraduates and graduates at Cambridge University, in the English Faculty, between January and March 1979.

In them, I tried to explain to that particular audience, at that particular time, some of the thinking, the experience and the aspirations that lay behind my work in the theatre during the last decade. Of course it is to be hoped that what are described are not only *my* thinking, experience, aspirations, but also – to a greater or lesser extent – those of many hundreds of other workers in alternative theatre during that period. It is to be hoped also that other people in other places will find the talks approachable and of some use.

They were made possible in the first place by the generosity of the Judith E. Wilson Fund, through which the Faculty Board of English in Cambridge was able to create a Visiting Fellowship with the aim of bringing practising theatre-people and/or poets into contact with the undergraduates, and vice-versa. To the late Judith E. Wilson, her Trustees, and the Faculty Board of English I am truly grateful. My thanks must also go to the Master and Fellows of Trinity Hall, Cambridge, who took me in, housed me and fed me. A particular gratitude must go to Raymond Williams for the inspiration of his work and his conversation, and the kindness he has continued to give, and to Peter Holland for his friendship, practical help, and his enthusiasm.

There are two groups of people to whom I would like to dedicate this book. The first is those students in Cambridge who attended these talks, and who gave me so much back, in discussion and argument, both inside the lecture-room and outside it. The second group is those – company-members and audience – who have shared the experience of making 7:84's kind of theatre, who have also given me so much, in the realms of the imagination, creation, wit, experience of life and work, of politics, and of the history of the labour movement – in rehearsal rooms, theatres, clubs, community centres and bars throughout the land. May both groups never lose contact with each other

Liverpool, 1st May 1981

Behind the Clichés
of Contemporary Theatre

I imagine I am here today to reflect on my practice as a writer and director (and stagehand) in the theatre and to pass on the benefit of these reflections every Wednesday afternoon. This process can become autobiographical, egocentric, even at times megalomaniac, but if you wish a more measured, 'objective' approach, I cannot oblige. Try Bernard Levin – due to industrial action, I believe, he has suddenly become available.

By the way, the sub-title of these lectures is: 'Contemporary Theatre and the *Mediation* of Reality'. It is not the *Meditation* of Reality as announced in the Cambridge University Lecture list – a misprint entirely appropriate to this place of learning. I am trying to discuss a more active intervention by the theatre in forming contemporary life and contributing to the future of our society.

I could have called them 'Telling the Story' – because that's what theatre does. You go into a space, and some other people use certain devices to tell you a story. Because they have power over you, in a real sense, while you are there, they make a choice, with political implications, as to which story to tell – and how to tell it.

But we go in, watch their story, and come out, changed. If their work is good, and skilfully written, pre-

sented and acted, we come out feeling exhilarated: we are
more alive for seeing it, more aware of the possibilities of
the human race, more fully human ourselves. So far, so
wonderfully universal. But this story we watch can have a
meaning: a very specific meaning. What if we are black,
say, and we go to see some splendidly effective, but completely racist theatre show? What if we are Jewish, and go
to see a piece of anti-semitic drama such as one could
easily see in Germany in the 1930s? Are we quite so exhilarated? Quite so fully human? Or would we not feel
demeaned, excluded from humanity, diminished in our
possibilities and a great deal more pessimistic about the
future of the human race than when we went in? The
meaning, and value, of theatre can clearly change from
country to country, group to group, and – significantly –
from class to class.

What does this mean then? That not *all* stories are so
wonderfully universal? That the political and social
values of the play cannot be the same for one audience as
they are for another? What a terribly confusing state of
affairs!

How can you know where you stand? How can you be
suitably academic, objective and withdrawn? How can
you make a universally valid *judgement*?

It is next to impossible to take the existence of various
different audiences into account, to codify their possible
reactions to a piece of theatre, to evaluate a piece of
theatre from *within several frameworks*. So what do we do?
Well, I'll tell you what most of us do – we take the point of
view of a *normal* person – usually that of a well-fed, white,
middle class, sensitive but sophisticated literary critic:
and we *universalize* it as *the* response.

The effect of such a practice is to enshrine certain
specific values and qualities of a play above others. For
example, mystery – or mysteriousness as it so often

becomes. How often has this 'all-pervading air of mystery' been praised by critic and academic alike, from Yeats's *Purgatory* down through Beckett to our own cut-price product, Harold Pinter? Mystery, the ingredient that leavens the loaf – or should I say makes the dough rise?

But many audiences don't like mystery, in that sense of playing games with knowledge, and words, and facts. They become impatient, they want to know what the story is meant to be about, what is supposed to have happened. They wish a different order of mystery. But because we have universalized the critical response to 'mystery' that proclaims it as a truly wonderful thing, we now have to dismiss those audiences as philistine, as outside true theatre culture, as – and this is the Arnold Wesker refinement – in need of education. My belief, and the basis of my practice as a writer in the theatre for the last ten years, has been that there *are* indeed different kinds of audiences, with different theatrical values and expectations, and that we have to be very careful before consigning one audience and its values to the critical dustbin. Unfortunately, almost all the current assumptions of critical thought do precisely that, by universalizing white middle-class sensitive but sophisticated taste to the status of exclusive arbiter of a true art or culture. I intend to devote the third of these lectures to a more detailed analysis of the differences of value between the two main kinds of theatre audience in this country, the 'educated' middle-class audience, and the 'philistine' working-class audience. For the time being let me just note that there is indeed a difference, and that I do not accept the following assumptions:

1. that art is universal, capable of meaning the same to all people;
2. that the more 'universal' it is, the better it is;

3. that the 'audience' for theatre is an idealized white, middle-class, etc., person and that all theatre should be dominated by the tastes and values of such a person;

4. that, therefore, an audience without such an idealized person's values is an inferior audience; and

5. that the so-called 'traditional values' of English literature are now anything other than an indirect cultural expression of the dominance over the whole of Britain of the ruling class of the south-east of England.

cf Island of the mighty

To be more specific, I *do* believe that there is a working-class audience for theatre in Britain which makes demands, and which has values, which are different from those enshrined in our idealized middle-class audience. That these values are no less 'valid' – whatever that means – no less rich in potential for a thriving theatre-culture, no thinner in 'traditions' and subtleties than the current dominant theatre-culture, and that these values and demands contain within them the seeds of a new basis for making theatre that could in many ways be more appropriate to the last quarter of the twentieth century than the stuff that presently goes on at the National Theatre, or at the Aldwych.

Having planted the revolutionary suggestion that middle-class theatre is not by definition the only, or even necessarily the best, kind of theatre, I would like to complicate matters further by talking a little about the 'language' – as they say – of theatre.

Why is the question of the 'language' of theatre a problem? First, let us glance at recent cinema criticism. Here we see a fairly clear consensus, whatever may be the opinions about it, on the subject of the 'language' of cinema. The 'language' of cinema includes the text, the *mise-en-scène*, the lighting, the editing, the locations, the performances, the casting, the camera angles, the use of filters, the music, the effects-track, the framing – in short, everything that is communicated by the reels of celluloid which make up the experience of cinema when adequately projected.

Theatre, however, is still discussed as if it were a book. Now I hope I don't need to say that there does exist a huge body of *dramatic literature*, which is rarely performed and whose 'language' is indeed that of words on the page – and it is far from inadequate as a source of immense literary pleasure.

And of course there is no doubt that words constitute a major element in the language of theatre. But I would remind you that words, the text, may well not be a decisive element in theatre. In fact, the sum total of what happens on the stage may not, in extreme circumstances, be decisive, as Mrs Lincoln once remarked.

I must emphasise that the language of theatre is possibly even more extensive than that normally ascribed to cinema. For not only must the text, *mise-en-scène*, lighting, performances, casting, music, effects, placing on the stage all be taken into account in order to arrive at a description of the stage event, but also the nature of the audience, the nature, social, geographical and physical, of the venue, the price of tickets, the availability of tickets, the nature and placing of the pre-publicity, where the nearest pub is, and the relationships between all these considerations themselves and of each with what is happening on stage. For when we discuss theatre, we are discussing a social event, and a very complex social event, with a long history and many elements, each element also having a long and independent history.

To complicate matters further, each occasion of theatre is different, evanescent and impossible to record. Of course this does not reduce us to silence. But what it does do all too often is to reduce the language of theatre that is studied academically to the most easily obtainable – the words. Perhaps that study will include pictures of the set or leading actors, and descriptions of the theatre building, but, above all, it will be concerned with the words said to have been uttered on the stage. You can buy them in a book, they never change, they are convenient objects of study. But words are not the 'language' of theatre, and by exclusively attending to them we reduce, improverish the event for academic convenience. The act of *creating theatre* has nothing to do with the making of dramatic literature: dramatic literature is what is sometimes left behind when theatre has been and gone. Above all, it is fatal for playwrights to try to write 'dramatic literature'. Some do fall into the trap, for example Edward Bond's recent plays which to me smack more of posterity-hunting than theatre-making. At this point in the history of theatre, I believe playwrights are forced to make it their business to 'write' or 'make' not only a text, not only a production, not only an atmosphere, but the whole language of the *event* of theatre. Why? Because so much of the language we inherit is dead, or deadening. Because the inherited language is based on so many moribund assumptions. A serious playwright today must work with *all* the elements of the language of the theatrical event – he or she must reinvent theatre every time he or she writes a play: the whole theatre, not just what is said on stage. The simple acceptance of, say, the location of the event, the kind of publicity available, the price of admission and the behaviour of the box office staff as all being someone else's problem, and not areas of personal concern for creative artists means that in effect a great deal of the meaning of the event socially and politically is taken away from the writer. The play itself can completely change its meaning, given the wrong theatre or wrong publicity, or even the wrong ticket prices.

There are elements in the language of the theatre beyond the text, even beyond the production, which are often more decisive, more central to one's experience of the event than the text or the production. I wish to discuss several of these – notably the choice of venue, audience, performers, and the relationship between performer and audience – in later lectures. For the moment, let me declare that the constant reduction of the language of theatre to one of its elements, simply because that is more reproducible, and therefore more convenient for discussion, is not only misleading but dangerous.

Now one of the basic assumptions about the language of theatre, given the practice of 'universalizing' the expectations of the white middle-class sensitive but sophisticated ideal auditor, is that in order to change the meaning or class-orientation of theatre, all you need to do is to change the content of *some* of what happens on the stage.

For example, there is a whole generation of playwrights who began their writing careers at the Royal Court theatre between 1956 and 1966, who have gone on to create what is in fact the current dominant mode of theatre, and who are said to have allowed the voice of the working class into the British theatre for the first time since Shakespeare, or even the Mystery plays. As Martin Esslin puts it: 'plays dealing with lower-class characters speaking a non-standard English and flouting the conventions of the "who's for tennis" school of playwriting could actually become profitable theatrical ventures'.

I should like to devote part of this first lecture to looking at the work done at the Royal Court during that decade, because those years were crucial and formative for what is now the mainstream of British theatre. Various shifts and changes took place at the Court during that time which have become automatic assumptions today.

I shall not attempt a potted history of how the Royal Court was founded, or indeed how it was able to continue – for those who are interested this is quite adequately documented in *Playwrights' Theatre* by Terry Browne. What I am interested in is what is vulgarly called 'Post-Osborne Drama'. It is an appalling phrase, but one not without meaning, since John Osborne was the first of a line of young, 'lower class', native-born and educated, British dramatists whose work was encouraged and presented by the English Stage Company at the Royal Court. This line includes: Michael Hastings, N. F. Simpson, John Arden, Ann Jellicoe, Arnold Wesker, Donald Howarth, Willis Hall, Alun Owen, Christopher Logue, Harold Pinter, Edward Bond, Henry Livings, Charles Wood, Christopher Hampton, Howard Brenton, David Storey, David Halliwell and Joe Orton.

The writing of these playwrights has come to be the dominant way of 'mediating contemporary reality' of our theatre. They, and their imitators on television, radio and film, are the people who tell the story, in the dramatic forms.

In 1956 John Osborne is said to have inaugurated a New Era; Revitalised various things; Heralded a new Dawn; Opened the Doors of the Theatre to this, that and the other – (mostly the northern working class) and 'Given a New Direction' to British theatre. Subsequent to this amazing 'Open Sesame', many more than forty thieves have entered the cave full of gold and treasures and dipped their fingers into the oaken chests. Many another young writer has followed Osborne into the Royal Court or the Aldwych or the National Theatre. They have been served by an array of talented ex-working-class directors and actors, whose ranks are ever growing. Many of these writers, directors and actors have become both rich and successful – one thinks of John Dexter who directed Wesker's plays once, now at the Met in New York; or Albert Finney with his race horses; Tony Richardson in Hollywood, or Osborne himself, a crusty old eccentric in his club, yapping away about the trade unions ruining the country. All very powerful, influential figures.

More important, this particular *kind* of theatre has become equally respectable, conventional and pernicious. It has spread, or its influence and personnel have spread, into the Royal Shakespeare Company, the National Theatre, and almost all the major repertory theatres, into all areas of television and broadcasting, into many home-grown British films, even from time to time into Covent Garden Opera House. It is the Regular Route, one which I followed myself, for the north-country scholarship boy to take from the university into – ultimately – Harry Saltzman's mansion (in Uxbridge), or Sam Spiegel's big yacht steaming out of Monaco harbour into the Mediterranean sunset. How many times, how many eager young writers, actors, directors have taken their talent along to Sloane Square, or the Hampstead Theatre Club, or the Aldwych, or now the Cottesloe segment of the National Theatre complex, feeling a part of history, but more than that a certain loyalty to their own experience, a certain security in being progressive, even socialist if such is their desire, feeling that this kind of theatre is really significant.

Well of course it is, but it is just *what* it signifies that is the question. Its greatest claim to social significance is that it produced a new 'working-class' art, that it somehow stormed the Winter Palace of bourgeois culture and threw out the old regime and turned the place into a temple of workers' art. Of course it did nothing of the kind. What Osborne and his clever director Tony

Richardson had achieved was a method of translating some areas of non-middle-class life in Britain into a form of entertainment that could be sold to the middle classes. Similarly with Wesker, John Dexter's contribution as director of the trilogy was to shape the plays, the performances, the design and the overall mood into artefacts that London's trendier fashion-setters could come to and be titillated by. John Arden's *Live Like Pigs*, however, a relatively unmediated piece of raw life, was immensely unpopular, and the theatre nearly empty throughout its short run. *Epitaph for George Dillon*, of course, and *The Entertainer*, with Olivier quickly onto the band wagon, made a lot of money, and transferred to the West End where they made even more money. Then Arden's *Serjeant Musgrave's Dance* came on and drove them all out again, and lost the money.

I worked at the Royal Court on and off from June 1958 to sometime in 1961, writing a musical, working with a group of actors on a new rehearsal technique, and reading plays from the huge pile in the tiny dramaturgic office at ten bob a time. I remained in close touch through much of the 60s. The curious fantasy that the values of that place were anything other than bourgeois, élitist and utterly whimsical is a refinement which must have come later. What the Court was looking for was the theatrical *frisson*, the unusual talent exposing itself in an 'extraordinary moment', the presence of 'danger' on the stage, of the unpredictable, the over-stimulated, the hyper-thyroid, the abundantly vital. If this came from Peter O'Toole in *The Long and the Short and the Tall*, or Joan Plowright in Ionesco, or Patrick Magee in Beckett, or Wilfred Lawson in O'Casey, or Olivier in Osborne, or Michael Caine in Pinter, or Frank Finlay in Wesker, it was cherished not because of its class origin or significance, but because it was 'thrilling', i.e. new and stimulating.

I remember sitting in the second row of the circle watching David Storey's *The Contractor*, in Lindsay Anderson's production. During the course of the evening, the actors physically erected a marquee complete with floor, and – God help them – took it down again. I don't know whether this was meant to 'say something' about labour, its dignity or otherwise, but I clearly recall being shocked at such cavalier waste of human effort. But I was even more shocked, and enlightened, by the huge enjoyment of the experience manifested by a person in the first row of the dress circle, who turned out to be the managing director of a textile firm. Perhaps there is something ungenerous in my reaction to this experience of theatre, but it did in fact cause me to reflect on the real significance of the 'Post-Osborne' theatre, and to come to the conclusion that this famed New Era/Dawn/ Direction of British theatre was no more than the elaboration of a theatrical technique for turning authentic working-class experience into satisfying thrills for the bourgeoisie.

Of course, the other great significance of this kind of theatre is supposed to be that it 'changed' the audience for theatre. No longer, we are told, was the theatre the haunt of black ties and evening gowns looking for simple philistine middle-class pleasures. This is not entirely true. The Royal Court has always had 'successful' productions, when the aforementioned black-tie brigade came in hordes, undisguised, and 'unsuccessful' productions when they stayed away, along with everyone else. But there *was* a leavening of turtle-necked, scowling young men and girls with coloured stockings who represented the 'new' audience – university-educated, perhaps in origin non-middle class, perhaps non-public school, perhaps even from Manchester. What these unprepossessing youths, of which I was one, were in fact doing was absorbing as many of the values of the middle class as possible, and contributing one or two new ones of their own to the re-formation of middle-class behaviour that was necessary if the middle class was to survive. In the 1950s there was a huge part of the British middle class which thought it had got back to living in the 1930s, when servants were cheap and did as they were told. As the Empire went, and the unions grumbled, and in 1956 the Suez adventure put paid to Britain's last fantasy that it could pillage the world at will by force of arms, so it became clear that the British middle class must change. We were the agents of that change. But in true British fashion, just as the aristocracy had managed between 1660 and 1800 to absorb, penetrate and largely become the rising bourgeoisie, so the middle classes in the 50s and 60s absorbed and penetrated the bright young working-class youth, thrown up by the 1944 Education Act in appreciably large numbers, and ... lo! after a short while, we were them.

In other words, the 'new' audience for this kind of theatre was, if not in origin certainly in ultimate desti-nation, merely a 'new' bourgeoisie, mingling in with the old, even indulging in miscegenation.

Let us look at a theatrical event at the Royal Court, a Sunday night production without décor of a new play in, say, 1960. The director will be one of the three or four as-sociates – Lindsay Anderson, John Dexter, William Gaskill, possibly Anthony Page. The play will have been chosen, or picked up, by one of them, because he was excited by it. The author will have been brought to the attention of either George Devine or one of these direc-tors by an agent, a critic, or some personal contact, perhaps via a university connection or an introduction effected by an actor, or another writer. Rarely will the play have been an unsolicited manuscript, read with oaths of joy by a ten-bob-a-time reader. Even if it had been, it would have stood no chance of production unless one of the directors had been thrilled by it.

The actors will be paid two pounds each for the whole thing, rehearsal (for ten days or two weeks) and performance. They will accept this token fee because they wish to ingratiate themselves with the Royal Court family, to become a Royal Court actor, to meet the directors, writers and casting director (source of much future employment at a more profitable rate) and to be seen by the audience. The actors will usually be of lower middle-class or middle-class origins, rarely working class, but often from the north or Wales or even the East End, will have done two years at drama school and be on the look-out for good work and good money. They will be in a highly competitive profession, and be good at using *all* the necessary devices to 'get on', even to pretending to be more working class than they really were.

The audience is fairly recognizable. In the centre of the front row of the circle sits George Devine, the benign headmaster, connected via Michel St Denis, with whom he worked, with the experimental theatre of the 30s in Paris and London (incidentally, St Denis was the nephew of Copeau of the Vieux-Colombier). Through his own career Devine knew many of the leading figures of the London theatre establishment, and through his teaching practice had worked with many of the best of the younger actors in London. Around him in the circle are the associate directors, already in demand for bigger, more commercial projects, together with a few chosen writers and friends, plus the designers, casting director, dramaturge, etc. Amongst them sit the businessmen, solicitors and their wives who 'support' the theatre, who raise and contribute money – for this is before the time of realistic Arts Council subsidies.

In the stalls are found the agents for plays and actors, the smart radio and television producers, the directors of other theatres, the film company casting directors, the brighter young film producers and directors – and of course the other actors and aspiring writers and directors who wish to catch the eye of some or all of the above. Plus the critics, poised to flee the theatre, the more quickly to create a new reputation, to destroy an ambition. And, of course, there are the talent-scouts for the German agents, the American managements, the Dutch, French, Norwegian theatres and agencies, anxious to earn their modest retainers by recommending the new British *wunderkind* before their rivals. In short, in the stalls are the ingenuous captains of an industry, the entrepreneurs of the new international culture market, the buyers and sellers, the purveyors of acceptable theatrical experience to the bourgeoisie of the Western world; with their approval, or at least their recognition of a more general approval, the tender sliver of the author's fantasy or experience so cheaply mounted on to this stage, could turn into a commodity, an international sensation, a property worth perhaps half a million dollars to the author, much more to the Broadway manager or film producer lucky enough to buy it.

Behind the *cognoscenti* in the front rows of the circle, and up in the upper circle, are the unknown public – the students, young actors, technicians, schoolmasters, theatre freaks, the innocently interested and the green-eyed aspirant who on the whole create the throng necessary to admire, first of all, the rest of the audience, and then even the play itself. From their ranks will come the future, and the approval that justifies the present – and pays for it.

Such, in my experience, was the kind of audience that went to the Royal Court, the 'post-Osborne' audience. I have dwelt upon it not in order to be rude to the Royal Court, but to try to indicate something about the characteristics of the experience of what has *now* come to be the mainstream of British theatre in the eyes of those who pronounce upon our culture. The work of Osborne, Pinter, Bond, Wesker, Arden, and their heirs – Stoppard, Griffiths, Brenton, Hare and Keeffe – may now seem to have developed beyond, say *Saved*, or *The Dumb Waiter*, or *The Kitchen*. But it is important to realize their aesthetic/social roots. The audience has changed very little in the theatre, the social requirements remain constant, the values remain firmly those of acceptability to a metropolitan middle-class audience, with an eye to similar acceptability on the international cultural market.

*   *   *

The tradition created among the European bourgeoisie by Ibsen, Strindberg, Chekhov, Shaw, Galsworthy, Anouilh, Cocteau, Giraudoux, Pirandello became a strong and self-confident tradition. It declared, without too much bother, that the best theatre is about the problems and the achievements of articulate middle-class men and sometimes women, is performed in comfortable theatres, in large cities, at a time that will suit the eating habits of the middle class at a price that only the most determined of the lower orders could afford, and will generally have an air of intellectuality about it – something to exercise the vestiges of one's education on and to scare off the Great Unwashed. There will be critics to make it more important by reviewing it in the important newspapers, and learned books written about it to prove that it really *is* 'art'.

The tradition of this kind of theatre in Britain runs in some kind of unspoken competition with the same traditions in other advanced capitalist nation-states, and therefore we loyally identify it as ours, which is better than theirs. It *is* British Drama: it had defined itself as such, just as Kevin Keegan defined himself as England's contribution to European football.

*   *   *

From even a brief examination of the elements of the 'event' of theatre, we can see clearly that when the 'post-Osborne' British dramatists set out to 'tell the story', to mediate contemporary reality, they were already inflected towards an account that would be acceptable to the middle class. Much as they may have thought that they had introduced the authentic voice of the working class into the theatre, as I'm sure did Wesker, Alun Owen, Edward Bond, Arden and even Pinter, the message that voice was trying to carry was inevitably swamped by the many other tongues of the event.

Let me go back to my original observations about the non-universality of theatre. Although this 'post-Osborne' drama is now the dominant kind of drama in this country, it is not the only kind. While the audiences at the Royal Court were being 'thrilled' by watching actors pretend to be workers actually working, the other traditions of theatre were not dead. The West End went on being the West End, with Robert Morley in comedies about the troubles of businessmen, and *Salad Days*, and *My Fair Lady*. Many variety theatres were still going in 1956, but they were closing down, almost one a week: the cinema had finally taken over. But the variety performers were moving into the working men's clubs, and the social clubs, and still doing summer seasons and panto which flourished. In the late 40s, Joan Littlewood, Gerry Raffles, Ewan MacColl and a few other socialists had formed various companies to tour with socialist plays before working-class audiences, in Scotland, around Manchester and eventually in the Theatre Royal, Stratford, in East London. There were several Unity theatres, mostly amateur, though some for a time professional, which were closely connected with the Communist Party, and which put on agitational and other socialist plays to working-class audiences. In other words, another, different story was being told. Reality was being mediated in several very different ways.

2

Towards a Working-Class Theatre

In the first lecture I discussed the role of the Royal Court theatre between 1956 and 1970, and suggested that on the whole it was an expression not of a new working class, but of an old middle class trying to renew itself. One of the methods of doing this was, and is, to give an ear to working-class writers, and their experience. But this method is only successful when the resulting work is translated in production into something remote but thrilling for the London middle class. Also, I argued, the 'language' of theatre is made up of much more than simply the words on the page or even the actions on the stage: and the language the Royal Court spoke was the language of a small metropolitan cultural group with developing but essentially bourgeois values. As the *kind* of theatre introduced by and elaborated at the Royal Court is now the dominant kind of theatre in England, it is commonly assumed that its values – developing but essentially bourgeois – are those of theatre as a whole; that the tastes of a white, well-fed, sensitive but sophisticated literary critic may be universalized into the eternally valid good taste of theatre, be defined as Art; and that all theatrical battles are to be fought on this terrain. In opposition to this idealist view of Art and the Theatre, I suggested a more materialist way of looking at it as an evanescent, unrecordable act of communication between two groups of people present in person in the same space on the same night; and that the communication took place in many areas including the price of tickets and the content of the programme. And, finally, I suggested that there were conventions of entertainment and theatre-making which were working class rather than middle class, which contained greater potential than the 'post-Osborne' drama.

Before going on to discuss some of those conventions of entertainment, I should like to point briefly to the relevance of this discussion to the subject of these lectures, the mediation of reality in contemporary theatre.

It would be very easy to dismiss such a discussion as mere formalism of an inverted kind. 'Form, as such, has no meaning', is the charge – indeed, the 'content' ought to determine the form. Now in the theatre these attitudes are wrong and dangerous, because elements of the form are taken quite clearly as signifiers of class content, either of exclusion of certain people or inclusion in the overall ritual of the event. Tom Stoppard's recent piece of right-wing propaganda, for example, *Every Good Boy Deserves Favour*, requires a small symphony orchestra on stage. Now not only is there a relationship between the specific kind of culture that created the symphony orchestra – I mean the nineteenth-century industrial ruling class's idea of culture – and the reactionary 'message' of the piece – that socialism drives people mad – but also the orchestra itself signifies exclusion. It is almost comic that Stoppard has noticed popular theatre going round with little rock-groups, signifying to large numbers of working-class youths that there might be something in the show for

them, and he has almost translated this into the presence
of the LSO, thereby reassuring large numbers of the
middle-class middle-aged that there might well be something in the show for them – as indeed there is. The
devices and conventions of theatre are very much part of
the language, and can, at times, be decisive. They do
indeed have meaning, quite apart from that they 'carry' in
terms of 'content'. And in the case of bourgeois theatre,
the meaning of these devices and conventions is most frequently one which supports the cultural, social, political
and economic dominance of the ruling and middle
classes, and is hostile to the growth to full cultural maturity of – and of course any increase in the political power of
– the working class. Now this is quite a serious message to
be putting across before you have even written your play.
As I indicated last week, it can often be a message which
cancels out the meaning of the 'content' of an apparently
'progressive' piece of writing, or at least creates enough
contradictions and confusions to render it meaningless.
It is a message to which I, and many others, are opposed.

Perhaps it would be valuable to clarify one or two political points. I can see no way of discussing contemporary
theatre, or the way reality is mediated, without the par-
ticipants in the discussion declaring, or at least being
aware of, their political position. A minimal statement of
my own position might be summarised as follows: ours is
a class society, and, notwithstanding the welfare state,
nationalisation, the TUC and the Labour Party, the class
which owns, controls or manages private capital and state
capital is a coherent social entity with immense power;
the British state and its institutions are organized in the
interests of that ruling class, which is supported in its position of power by intermediate classes dependent upon
the social order it creates for their well-being and their

superiority over the working class, i.e. the middle and professional classes, and the petty bourgeoisie; and all these classes combine to reproduce this system because it works in their interest, and the most effective way to reproduce the system is to create an overpowering ideology which penetrates all areas of the individual consciousness, in order to legitimate class rule and maintain it. I see the bourgeois theatre in all its forms as part of that legitimating ideology. In opposition there are sections of, or individuals within, all the above groups and classes: they are, however, powerless without the main opposition group, those who are in fact exploited, – economically, physically, medically, culturally, socially – the much maligned working class.

The interests of this class are in contradiction to those of the ruling class, who need more production for less money in order to survive in a competitive world market. The working class in Britain expresses its opposition most vociferously in terms of cash, simple economist demands which have suceeded to some extent in raising the level of material welfare of many workers and their families. But these ignore those other forms of deprivation and exploitation, which actually keep the working class in an inferior position and perpetuate the class structure of late capitalism. This area of social, political and cultural development of the working class towards maturity and hegemony, leading to the possibility of a classless society at some time in the future, is that in which an oppositional form of theatre can, and does, play its part. It is, in my opinion, a form of theatre which is searching, through the experience and forms of the working class, for those elements which point forward in the direction of a future rational, non-exploitative, classless society, in which all struggle together to resolve humanity's conflict with nature, and to allow all to grow to the fullest possible experience of life on earth. But it would be Utopianism, political and cultural, to imagine that the art of such a classless society can be produced without a long phase of struggle and development, which we are deep within at this moment.

To create a kind of theatre that tells the story from a different perspective, in a language that a different group of people understand, i.e. to create a working-class form of theatre appropriate to the late twentieth century, we have to look at the language of working-class entertainment, at least to see what kind of language it is.

Perhaps we could plunge straight into a working-men's club in Chorlton-cum-Hardy, an inner suburb of Manchester in, say, 1963. A barn of a place, looking from the outside not unlike a nineteenth-century institution, asylum, poorhouse, or some such, it is painted over manfully with grey-green paint, with a few billboards set strategically on the walls failing to advertise the coming attraction. It announces itself over the doorway, plus 'Members Only', a fair warning if ever there was one. The surrounding landscape is dual-carriageway light-industrial, with an infill of ancient red-brick terraces, with people living in them, mostly industrial workers and their families. Some are now heading for the club. In the hallway there is a heavy challenge as to club membership. The club is privately owned, and has a licence which must be safeguarded. Also in the foyer stands a row of fruit machines. In the hall itself, one wall is completely opened up as a bar. There are perhaps twelve to fourteen men in white jackets ferrying drinks from the bar to the tables, and three or four women serving behind the bar. All drinks are ordered and brought to the tables by order of the management. Tables occupy most of the floor-space, with between four and sixteen chairs per table, altogether maybe 400 seats. At one end of the hall is the stage, a small patch, raised only a few feet, most of it occupied by a massive electronic organ. A few plastic flowers and a stand holding a microphone separate it from the dance-floor, again quite small, immediately below. In the centre of the hall, unlit, a large wrestling ring.

The audience coming in are dressed up, with ties and going-out frocks, but feel comfortable and glad to be out of working clothes. They are not intimidated by the man on the door, nor anyone else for that matter, the club is for them, is, in a real sense, 'theirs'. And yet, important to note, in another sense it is there to exploit them and their needs. The clubs sell a lot of beer, and are courted by the brewers, so much so that some club comittees or social secretaries are bribed to take So-and-so's ales. In other clubs there is a sense of consumers banding together to get what they want, which is quite interesting. I ought to explain that some clubs are privately owned, by a small businessman, or even a brewery. Others are owned by the membership and run by 'the committee', with a lot of power in the hands of the chairman, the treasurer, and the social secretary. They tend to be very autocratic, and very demanding. One social secretary in a club in Bedwas, in South Wales, told me with pride, 'We're the only club in the world to have sacked Tom Jones – twice!' They often distribute high fees, for artists who go down well with the members – not necessarily the famous or the TV stars, sometimes local acts, sometimes retired variety stars like Tessie O'Shea, or Johnny Ray. There is a sense of power and confidence about the clubs, with a whiff of petty corruption, and seedy materialistic hedonism that relates directly to the economism of the British trades unions and the pragmatism of the British Labour Party.

What is the entertainment? Well, first there's the booze – lots of it, at club prices, i.e. a bit cheaper than the pub.

Then there is seeing and being seen, chatting and meeting friends. But on a more formal level, there's Ernie, the MC, clubland's answer to Steve Ovett, already producing rich electronic sounds and coy rhythms from the big Wurlitzer on stage. By seven o'clock the crowd is quite big, and Ernie is doing a warm-up, telling a few gags, then introducing the first performer – 'Give him a big hand!' – an up-and-coming comedian/crooner or young girl who bounces around singing pop songs merrily, all teeth and tulle. Then Ernie will come on, after a ten-to fifteen-minute act, and sing himself, or tell more stories, then bring on another couple of early-evening acts – a group of young lads singing, not too loud, or another comic or vocalist or a ventriloquist. Ernie accompanies all of these on the organ, operates the lights for them, introduces them and sees them off. Then: the moment you've all been waiting for, Ernie wheels on the bingo machine, and cards are sold around the tables. For half-an-hour, bingo, and more booze. The concentration on the bingo is, however, total. By now, the hall is pretty full, the atmosphere getting volatile and a bit loud. Among shrieks of excitement the bingo prizes are won. Ernie announces a ten-minute break before the wrestling. By now it's almost nine o'clock, and the booze is flying over the bar in gallons.

Suddenly, Ernie reappears, plays an electronic fanfare, dashes to the lightingboard, dramatically puts the lights up on the ring in the centre, leaps into it, seizes a microphone and becomes announcer for the wrestling, and soon, indeed, the referee.

The first lot of wrestling, two bouts, takes half-an-hour or so. Tempers flare, excitement, almost hysteria, rises as the stage-managed brutality, the melodramatic aggression works on the audience. With the promise of more to come, Ernie switches the action back to the stage. A swift change of lighting, a disc ready on the turntable, and Ernie announces the beautiful Carmencita – in reality a raw young red-head from Stockport – who comes on and proceeds to strip, with great encouragement from the single males, but little finesse. She has been 'trained' by an agent in Manchester, who now takes a large slice of her fee, and in return gets her bookings around the area. When she has unconvincingly ground to a halt, G-string intact except on stag nights, she scampers off, and Ernie comes on to announce the next week's attractions, and maybe the comedian and the singer will come back for a second spot. Then the second session of wrestling is under way – this time more violent, more hysteria-inducing. It leaves the audience aroused, aggressive and largely drunk. Ernie then plays dance music on the Wurlitzer, the dance floor gets crowded, the fights break out, the glasses smash, and the white-coated waiters turn out to be a squad of bouncers in disguise. By ten-thirty the crowd is out on the street, going home after a night out, singing, laughing, arguing, fighting: an average, twice-a-week gala night in Chorlton-cum-Hardy in the '60s, and, with very few variations, in the '70s too.

Is this, then, working-class entertainment, the raw material of a future proletarian theatre? Well, it's not the only kind of working-class entertainment, nor the best. It bears all the marks of the suffering of the urban industrial working class of the north of England – the brutality, the violence, the drunkenness, the sexism, the authoritarianism that have been part of its life since the Industrial Revolution. On the other hand, it is not, as some might think, a night in outer darkness: it is a night in inner Manchester, enjoyed by many people who in themselves have many excellent qualities. These are the people who may well be making revolution. It will bear a certain amount of examination.

What I would like to do at this point is to illustrate a typical programme of a Blue Blouse Theatre Group presentation. They flourished in Russia between 1919 and 1928, when, significantly, they were closed down. Here is a description of their activities:

The repertoire of *Blue Blouse* was mainly based on actual socio-political events presented in a manner designed to interest and amuse a large audience. The performance lasted for about an hour and a half. It opened with a parade in which the whole company was presented on stage, and the parade was followed, at a brisk tempo, by a montage of ten to fifteen different numbers (attractions) using various forms and techniques.

1. *The dramatic forms*: monologue, dialogue, mass declamation, sketches with domestic and international themes that were usually treated comically. A special type of presentation was the oratorium – dramatic singing at the end of which the actors constructed symmetrical forms or symbols such as a star or a factory complex. (The skit 'Industrialization' described in *The Christian Science Monitor* is probably such an oratorium.)

2. *Forms derived from dance and gymnastics*: acrobatic dance and physical dance, both executed by two performers and usually accompanied by jazz. Collective dance based on the movement of machines – for example, the movement of a pump or of a turning wheel – was the 'dance of the machine'. Purely physical exercises and gymnastic numbers (individual or collective) were also presented.

3. *Techniques derived from the plastic arts*: the animated poster and the poster composition. In the former, a huge poster was placed on stage; holes had been cut in appropriate places for the heads, arms and legs of the actors, who put themselves into the poster and recited the text. The latter was an arrangement of posters and symmetrically positioned actors.

4. *Musical numbers*: popular and folk songs, often involving topical satire, and the playing of instruments

such as the accordion.

5. *Film*: actual bits of film or slides were rarely used. A special technique was the kino review (also called 'living film' or 'electrified theatre'). During the performance of a skit, projectors with turning filters were used to create a flickering effect and the impression of a film projection.

In the montage of numbers, the emphasis was on their variety. The spoken forms were followed by dances, gymnastic or musical numbers; the propaganda numbers were followed by more entertaining material. The performance concluded with an 'ending parade' in which the company summarized the performance, commenting upon its political message but also on themselves and on the *Blue Blouse* in general.

Aside from socio-political content, the requirements on the text from a formal point of view were: 'The text must be clear and sharp without unnecessary words. It should resemble the speech of a good orator, and the poems of Mayakovsky, Aseyev and Tretyakov.'

Now the Blue Blouse theatre movement was clearly very conscious of popular forms, as well as being influenced by the impeccably bourgeois experiments of Futurism, both directly from the work of Marinetti, and by way of productions by Meyerhold and Eisenstein. The productions were not tame mouthpieces of the government, indeed they specialized in attacks on the stupidity and the dangerous nature of Soviet bureaucracy – but they *were* immensely popular. After the initial successes of the first Blue Blouse group, other groups were set up around the country to mount local variants on their shows. In January 1928 there were 484 professional companies and 8,000 amateur companies in the Blue Blouse movement. Clearly their kind of theatre, the form of their theatre, opened the doors to the people, and in they came. Clearly, too, there was a consonance between this form, and what the groups were saying to and, in a

real sense, *for* the people. And there are some interesting
consonances with the preferred *form* of the Chorlton-
cum-Hardy Gala Night. The characteristics of variety,
music, satire, physical action, immense energy, and sim-
plicity, or rather, non-elaborateness of presentation, are
features that will recur in almost all kinds of working-
class entertainment.

A gentler kind, with many of these characteristics, is
the Christmas panto. Here, of course, a certain elaborate,
not to say spectacular element in the presentation is traditional, and becomes more so as the years go by, often to
the detriment of other qualities. But panto adds a crucial
element to all the others: narrative. Somehow, through
all the comedians doing their spots, the ultra-violet
underwater fish-ballet, the lady with the white doves, the
pop singer who can't speak, the principal girl who can't
sing, the numb-faced little girls from the local dancing
classes, and the merry crash of over-ambitious scenery,
somehow there's a story, no matter how secondary its
role, usually a narrative from the folk tradition. It has
characters, incidents, amazing events, evil forces, good
forces, and a very pronounced morality in its resolution,
when the baddies die and the goodies turn into nuclear
families.

The panto throws up a new kind of relationship, that
between narrative and variety form. It is perfectly acceptable that a character should come on, introduce him or
herself to the audience, outline their predicament or
desire in the story, then proceed to tell a row of jokes
about Irishmen. Which is very interesting, for the audience, next time that character comes on, will remember
the plot point, and forget about the Irishmen. The performer, if any good at all, can establish a personal relationship with the audience which will allow him or her to
signal very clearly to them when it is time for a song or a

few gags that have got nothing to do with the plot, and they will deploy their imaginations accordingly. Now this whole process is much too difficult for a Royal Court audience – they would demand some consistent relationship with the fictional character, and in the absence of that find themselves very confused, and go off to complain about it. The *safety* of observing a distanced slice of life, or a poeticized piece of fantasy, is not necessary for a working-class audience on its home ground. The boldness of your experimentation with the inter-relationship between audience, actor and character is limited only by the confidence with which it is carried out. This is not, as some critics have thought, because the club/panto audience is unused to theatre, and therefore naively accepting – on the contrary, it is the sophistication of the audience of the folk tales, able to shift ground with ease if given secure guidance. Panto, as a form, also raises the question of localization of working-class culture, which I should like to discuss in the next lecture, when I would like to try to outline the main differences between working-class and middle-class forms of theatre. For the moment, before going back to Chorlton-cum-Hardy, let us look at some other forms of working-class entertainment.

The pop or rock concert has an increasing theatricality of presentation, and indeed offers all kinds of exciting possibilities, particularly when combined with audible lyrics, singers and musicians who can act, and a suitable story-line. Popular song, on record, radio, television, film soundtrack or live in concert, is obviously of major importance as an element of working-class entertainment. There are three possible reactions to it: mindless, related to the beat and the orchestration; musical, related primarily to the melody and harmonies; and multiple, related to paying attention to the lyric, the time, the performance, etc. and their inter-relationships. If you can achieve the last, as the Beatles often did, you are on the way towards something really interesting from the point of view of musical theatre. Given a musician/composer who can create popular music which is also musically complex and interesting, using sharp, imaginative lyrics, you have the miraculous flowering of Kurt Weill and Brect in the late 20s and early 30s, and their enduringly 'popular' songs, and their musical plays and opera. In the music of Weill – perhaps more than anywhere in the theatre – has my thesis of the potential development of a more mature, richer, more confident culture springing from and related to popular forms of entertainment, been exemplified.

Of course, the working class has responded most avidly to the new media – films, television, and gramophone records in particular – while the middle classes held back for many years after each innovation, in a rather conservative attitude, believing that Coward and Rattigan were more artistically valid than, say, Bunuel or Eisenstein, because Coward and Rattigan worked in a more ancient medium.

Within the cultural experience, and lingering in the language of the working class, come the silent movies; the talkies – westerns, thrillers, musicals, dramas, the lot – and, of course, the tidal flow of television. Now I believe that both film and television are of major importance in themselves as nodal points of the cultural development of the working class, and later I should like to discuss them both, but for the moment I'd prefer to see them as relating to the people's expectations from theatre.

The most obvious feature of popular films, silent or otherwise, is the pace and movement of the story-line. I think that I personally learnt more about writing for a popular audience from having my screenplays butchered time and time again by Harry Saltzman – one of the producers of the Bond films – or, on a different level, by Fred Zinnemann – producer/director of *A Man for all Seasons*, *Julia*, and above all, *High Noon*. These two, and some of the other producers and directors of crude, vulgar commercial movies know more about pace and movement than almost any author since Homer: they may, of course, have deficiencies in other areas. The level of plot invention per line, per page, per scene, is immensely high, much higher than most Post-Osborne playwrights would think at all necessary. It so happened that this level of intensity suits me very well, as I have always hated slack, romantic writing, and even more 'novel writing' in the theatre – the dull cruise through a scene to 'show' character or to 'create an atmosphere'. Working in films, as I did quite a lot between 1966 and 1972, taught me the need for, and some of the ways to get, pace and movement in a piece of theatre. What is perhaps more important, the experience of movies has led the popular audience to expect a certain level of invention and intensity and movement from a good piece of entertainment: and taught them the shorthand, the elliptical language of narrative necessary to maintain such a pace. What's more, the pace is increasing even over the last ten years – or at least the capacity of the language. I wrote a film in 1966, full of strange jump-cuts that moved the story along very fast. When it came out, many people claimed it confused them. I saw a re-run in 1972, with a normal sort of audience, and they had no trouble at all with the pace or the style of cutting. Television and other films had familiarized them with these techniques so that they could 'read' them as narrative devices which posed no great problem. I dare say it was partly because of these possibilities of pacing and jump-cutting that I decided I would tackle, in one play (*The Cheviot, the Stag and the Black, Black Oil*), some two hundred years of the history of the

Highlands of Scotland, and in *Lay off* the global complexities of the multinational corporations.

Another effect on popular audiences of so much film and television has been to create an awareness of very high standards of performance, in acting, comedy, music or movement, and in the techniques of presentation. In one way this 'definition' of high standards by the media has had definitely reactionary effects in some areas: the definition of women, for example, in terms of sterotypes, and the slick, pseudo-Las Vegas style of all the sub-Tom Jones singers who go round the clubs blowing the microphones. But the audiences can and do demand high standards from their entertainment, which is the beginning of the search for something better.

One of the characteristics of working-class culture as a whole is that it defines itself locally rather than nationally and continues to do so despite the standardization of all culture attempted by the mechanical media. This is not to say it has remained static in each area, or has become a source of nostalgia rather than on-going creation – although there is a great danger of that, particularly with the growth of commercial exploitation of 'folk-traditions' for the purposes of tourism, souvenir shop sales, and dim-witted light entertainment shows on television. Yet just as accents, dialects and in some parts of the UK even the language derive from the history of the area, and continue to grow and change and take in new words and phrases, so the popular culture of a locality stems from long-standing traditions, and it can grow, and adapt itself to absorb outside influence without losing its identity. This is as true of urban as of rural culture.

Therefore the *content* of the comedian's patter is likely to go down better if it refers to Manchester events and prejudices when in Chorlton-cum-Hardy. But it's not just the content of the gags that varies from place to place.

The 'feel' of an audience, the amount of communal cynicism, or cruelty, or sentimentality, or racism will vary
from place to place. The very form of entertainment will
be very different in a village hall in the Highlands and a
pub in a south London suburb – in terms of the time, the
music, the instruments, the pattern of events, the feel of
communication – though the differences are in fact being
decreased by television, the radio and the gramophone,
and one must recognise this fact of life. Nevertheless,
through the many different sub-cultures that make up
British working-class culture, there is a wide range of
entertainment forms, from the *ceilidh* in the Hebrides and
Highlands to the *noson llawen* in Wales, to the Talent
Night in the Dorset pub, from the Shetland fiddle-band
to the elephants in the circus. David Edgar, in a talk he
gave last year, dismissed the entire popular culture of the
UK as 'atrophied':

> It is true, for example, that remnants of the music hall tra-
> dition survive in club entertainment, but the grossly reac-
> tionary nature of the content of club acts is evidence that,
> though orientated towards the working class in form, the
> culture of the clubs has become bourgeois in essence (it is
> no coincidence that the uniform costume of club entertain-
> ers is the evening wear of the upper-middle-class).
>
> Some groups and companies have indeed drawn success-
> fully on other popular-cultural forms, but it is interesting
> that they have achieved most when they have employed
> forms actually peripheral to the urban British working
> class. Joan Littlewood's *Oh What a Lovely War*, for
> example, used the Pierrot show (a basically Italian form,
> translated into British seaside entertainment), and 7:84
> Scotland's use of the *ceilidh* form in *The Cheviot, the Stag
> and the Black Black Oil* succeeded precisely because it
> drew on a rural folk-form, and, indeed, was directed at
> audiences in the rural Highlands of Scotland.

One of David Edgar's problems, of course, is that in fact
he only saw *The Cheviot* on television, and he didn't see
the show 7:84 Scotland did after *The Cheviot*, called *The
Game's a Bogey*. This took precisely those grossly reactionary club show elements and, by a critical re-creation
of both form and content, produced a show of great
sophistication in artistic and political terms, which was
very far from being grossly reactionary, and which played
to packed and enthusiastic audiences in clubs in Scotland
not at all dissimilar to the very working-men's club in
Chorlton-cum-Hardy that we plunged into earlier. No,
Edgar is essentially wrong in this idealist distinction
between popular and populist – which are not opposites.
And he is equally wrong in thinking that the only true 'in
essence' (I quote) forms of popular culture are dying a
lingering death in the Celtic twilight.

I had hoped in this lecture to talk a little about the
school of theatre-making that has grown up in this
country that consciously uses the elements of popular
culture to create a theatre opposed to the values of the
post-Osborne drama and accessible to working-class
audiences. But that is a very large subject which I shall try
to deal with in the next lecture when I shall also be trying
to analyse some of the characteristics of this kind of
theatre. For the present, I shall finish with a quotation
from Franca Rame, an actress who works with and is
married to Dario Fò, one of Italy's most loved actor/
entertainers, who shocked the Italian theatre by leaving a
highly profitable touring theatre circuit, and a very
popular television show, in order to work in workers'
clubs. She is writing in the Preface to his Comedies
(1975):

> Audiences increased at every performance. From 1964 to
> 68 our box-office takings were always the highest among

the major companies in Italy and we were among those who kept the lowest prices. Yet it was just at the end of the 1968 season (a true record in terms of takings) that we arrived at the decision to leave the traditional structures of the official theatre. We had realised that, despite the hostility of a few, obtuse reactionaries, the high bourgeoisie reacted to our 'spankings' almost with pleasure. Masochists? No, without us realizing it, we were helping their digestion. Our 'whipping' boosted their blood circulation, like some good birching after a refreshing sauna. In other words we had become the minstrels of a fat and intelligent bourgeoisie. This bourgeoisie did not mind our criticism, no matter how pitiless it had become, through our use of satire and grotesque technique, but only so long as the exposure of their 'vices' occurred exclusively within the structures that they controlled. . . .

It was no longer enough to consider ourselves as democratic, left-wing artists full of sympathy for the working class and in general for the exploited. Sympathy was no longer sufficient. The lesson came to us directly from the extraordinary struggles of the working people, from the new impulse that the youth were giving in the schools to the fight against authoritarianism and social injustice, and for the creation of a new culture and a new relationship with the exploited classes. No longer could we act as intellectuals, sitting comfortably within and above our own privileges, deigning in our goodness to deal also with the predicament of the exploited. We had to place ourselves entirely at the service of the exploited, become their minstrels. Which meant going to work with the structures provided by the lower classes. This is why we immediately thought of the workers' clubs.

3

Mediating Contemporary Reality

In the first of these lectures I talked about the dominant forms of theatre today, their roots in the Royal Court theatre, and the class nature of that tradition. In the second lecture I described a night out at the Chorlton-cum-Hardy working-men's club, and various other forms of working-class entertainment.

Now there has been for some time a fairly clearly defined and quite extensive school of theatre-making which has its roots in the traditions of working-class entertainment. It has produced some theatre which is good by any standards. In my opinion it is not only the most important kind of theatre politically, but also theatrically, because the other kind of theatre is dying on its throne, dying of boredom, repetition, narrowness of interest, artistic and social confusion and banality compounded by a supreme self-importance. If you wish to verify that assertion, I suggest a visit to the National Theatre, any auditorium, any night, or a visit to the theatre in Cambridge, where this week you can catch the fruit of the work of the *National* Theatre, the *Oxford* Playhouse Company and the *Cambridge* Arts Theatre – what mighty intellectual institutions are invoked – yes, it's *Bedroom Farce* by Alan Ayckbourn, in a third-rate

hasn't
died
yet!

production with a crowd of actors, technicians, etc. who, I have no doubt, are all hoping to make it themselves onto the stages of the South Bank before too long. I don't imagine you will find the working classes, rural or urban, of Cambridge flooding in to catch the show.

The kind of theatre I am talking about obviously has its disaster areas as well, but on the whole plays to a much wider spectrum of the population. Its audience includes many sectors, notably from the working class, who have not been involved in theatre for many years, but who come now to the theatre as if for the first time. They bring fresh reactions, strong demands and a tremendous lack of self-consciousness, that, together with some creative theatre-making, can open the doors to many, many areas of theatre experience, and social/cultural experience, formerly denied not only to them but also to the theatre.

It is this area of theatre-making, with its roots in working-class entertainment, and drawing on a new audience, that I should like to examine now, and having looked briefly at its history and its present activities, I want to walk the tightrope by trying to define its qualities, and distinguish its differences from bourgeois theatre.

Let me say straight away that there is a complicating factor, which both confuses and enriches the issue. That is the tradition of Brecht and Piscator. I consider their kinds of theatre to be of immense value, but also to contain many contradictions. Brecht was immensely aware of form, and the impotence of the conventional theatre of the 20s in Germany to cope with the new subject matter with which the twentieth century was confronting it: 'Petroleum', said Brecht, 'resists the five-act form'. Piscator wrote in *Die rote Fahne* in 1928: 'The lack of any great imaginative writing which would express the present day with all its forces and problems is no accident but results from the complexity, dividedness and incompleteness of our age.' Piscator's solution was to 'smash the bourgeois dramaturgy' and set up his 'dramaturgical collective' to adapt not only novels but also other people's plays to suit the requirements of the new 'epic' theatre. This did not earn him the affection of many playwrights, but it *did* produce a way of 'making theatre' that used more elements of the 'language' of theatre than most of those writers could produce on a piece of paper. It meant that creative work in the area of staging or lighting could occur simultaneously with verbal or character work, and contribute to the overall meaning rather than be a decorative after-thought. We shall return to this way of working and its implications at a later stage; for the present let us simply note that Piscator became one of the first directors to use the stage as an equal source of meaning to the page.

Brecht in the 20s saw the way forward through new forms and new purposes in theatre:

Simply to comprehend the new areas of subject-matter imposes a new dramatic and theatrical form. Can we speak of money in the form of iambics? 'The Mark, first quoted yesterday at 50 dollars, now beyond 100, soon may rise, etc.' – how about that? Petroleum resists the five-act form; today's catastrophes do not progress in a straight line but in cyclical crises; the 'heroes' change with the different phases, are inter-changeable, etc.; the graph of people's actions is complicated by abortive actions; fate is no longer a single coherent power; rather there are fields of force which can be seen radiating in opposite directions; the power groups themselves comprise movements not only against one another but within themselves, etc., etc. Even to dramatize a simple newspaper report one needs something much more than the dramatic technique of a Hebbel or an Ibsen. This is no boast but a sad statement of fact. It is impossible to explain a present-day character by features or a present-day action by motives that would have been adequate in our fathers' time. We allowed ourselves (provisionally) not to inspect motives at all (for instance: *Im Dickicht der Städte, Ostpolzug*) in order at least not to impute false ones, and showed actions as pure phenomena by assuming that we would have to show characters for some time without any features at all, this again provisionally.

All this, i.e. all these problems, only bears on serious attempts to write *major* plays: something that is at present very far from being properly distinguished from common or garden entertainment.

Once we have begun to find our way about the subject-matter we can move on to the relationships, which at present are immensely complicated and can only be simplified by *formal* means. The form in question can however only be achieved by a complete change of the theatre's purpose. Only a new purpose can lead to a new art. The new purpose is called pedagogics.

Pedagogics. This was in 1929, and was followed by the *Lehrstück*, Brecht's shorter, instructional pieces, like *Lindbergh's Flight*, *The Measures Taken*, *He Who Said No*, *He Who Said Yes*, etc., plays with music which were taken to working-class districts to support the struggle within that class *for* Communism and *against* Hitlerism – so we are talking about Brecht at a time when his involvement with the Berlin workers was most urgent. But pedagogics is what he was offering them.

Perhaps it would help to look at Brecht's famous list of differences between *his* kind of theatre, Epic theatre, and what he called Dramatic theatre:

The modern theatre is the epic theatre. The following table shows certain changes of emphasis as between the dramatic and the epic theatre

DRAMATIC THEATRE	EPIC THEATRE
plot	narrative
implicates the spectator in a stage situation	turns the spectator into an observer, but
wears down his capacity for action	arouses his capacity for action
provides him with sensations	forces him to take decisions
experience	picture of the world
the spectator is involved in something	he is made to face something
suggestion	argument
instinctive feelings are preserved	brought to the point of recognition
the spectator is in the thick of it, shares the experience	the spectator stands outside, studies
the human being is taken for granted	the human being is the object of the inquiry
he is unalterable	he is alterable and able to alter
eyes on the finish	eyes on the course
one scene makes another	each scene for itself
growth	montage
linear development	in curves
evolutionary determinism	jumps
man as a fixed point	man as a process
thought determines being	social being determines thought
feeling	reason

What is perhaps most striking about that list – to me, anyway, as a theatre-maker – is its hostility to the audience. Pedagogics, after all, is the art of passing *down* information and judgements, the art of the superior to the inferior. Distance, in place of solidarity; pseudo-scientific 'objectivity' in place of the frank admission of a human, partisan and emotional perspective – coldness, in

McGrath departs from Brecht: Brecht condescends to audience

place of shared experience: politically, Stalinism rather than collectivism. (Which is not to imply that Brecht approved of the crimes of Stalin.)

Now it's not surprising that Brecht and Piscator showed such hostility to their audiences, as 98 per cent of the time they were the hated bourgeoisie. Piscator, for instance, was able to write that 'The masses have realised the importance of our theatre . . . Those who still see us merely as "the latest thing" will soon realise their mistake', at the same time as arranging to base his theatre in Berlin's West End and to operate on a scale which made the support of capitalist backers and a smart novelty-seeking audience essential. Certainly he reproached the workers more than once with their failure to support him better, but the conclusion he draws in *Das politische Theater*, that 'the proletariat, for whatever reason, is not strong enough to maintain its own theatre', was already the initial assumption of his planning. He was, in fact, trying to have things both ways – never a very good position for somebody who insists that the theatre must take sides.

Brecht satirized this sort of carry-on, for example, in a poem called 'The Theatre Communist'. He has denied that it is about Piscator, but it is relevant to the discussion since it points towards the contradictions not only of Piscator's but also of his own situation:

The Theatre Communist

A hyacinth in his buttonhole
On the Kurfürstendamm
This youth feels
The emptiness of the world.
In the W.C. it becomes clear to him: he
Is shitting into emptiness.

Tired of work
His father's
He soils the cafés
Behind the newspapers
He smiles dangerously.
This is the man who
Is going to break up this world with his foot like
A small dry cowpat.

For 3000 marks a month
He is prepared
To put on the misery of the masses
For 100 marks a day
He displays
The injustice of the world.

But here is a story, quoted by John Willett, about this same Brecht:

Fritz Sternberg the sociologist once described Piscator complaining how hard it was to set up a company in view of the high fees demanded by star actors. Brecht thereupon is supposed to have said 'they would act for me if I promised to give them extra rehearsals', taken the telephone and got a number of the leading Berlin actors promptly to agree to perform in a hypothetical production for less than they were asking Piscator.

I am not trying to make a point about their *personal* duplicity or hypocrisy, which would be very petty. The point is that both worked within a hierarchical commercial theatre structure, and they did so by choice. There were many smaller theatre groups at work in Germany through the 20s and early 30s, with direct contact with small working-class audiences: both Brecht and Piscator, in spite of professions to the contrary and occasional unsuccessful attempts to change things, were committed to working *within* the Berlin smart bourgeois theatre, albeit as 'oppositional' forces. Now this was, of course, connected with the difficulty of financing the size of theatre operation they envisaged, without an Arts Council or a Socialist state. It was also not unconnected with their intellectual and artistic formation, which was essentially that of the 'outsider' tradition within the mainstream of European high culture, and with which neither made a decisive break as their political opinions and consequent class sympathies shifted away from those appropriate to that tradition.

Interestingly enough, Brecht's Berliner Ensemble, created in East Germany after the 1939–45 war, retained many of the forms and structures of bourgeois theatre, and, now that Brecht has gone, is riven with rival factions fighting for control, and has virtually ceased to present *new* plays at all. It has become, in other words, an institution of power rather than creation: which I think is the contradiction at the heart of Brecht's theatrical ideology, and indeed of his politics and, as far as one can tell, of his personal life. Power, of course, is a necessary question for class politics of all kinds. I do not accuse Brecht of activity which is somehow 'outside his art' in being obsessed with power. There is a sense in which all cultural work which is at all conscious of class struggle *must* place the question of class power in the centre of its ideology. But I think that with Brecht the problem is that of displacing *class* power into a rather bourgeois form of artistic privilege, which does have certain correspondences with the political hierarchies of the Soviet Union and Eastern Europe.

However, the achievement of Brecht and Piscator in the area of political theatre on the side of the working class is beyond question. Their contribution to the 'language' of this kind of theatre is immense. But we must not confuse this vigorous inflection of bourgeois theatre with the creation of a working-class-based theatre, which I believe to be quite a different thing.

To turn now to the British theatre, and the growth of a tradition based on working-class forms, we have to begin with Joan Littlewood. As I am aware that most of you will never have seen her productions, and some may indeed only know her from her West End hits of the 60s, I'd like to quote, by way of introduction, from a piece by Ken Tynan. During the 60s I knew Tynan a little, and found the most impressive thing about him to be the quality and perceptiveness of his admiration for Joan Littlewood:

> Joan is given to talking in visionary riddles, like some latterday William Blake let loose on show business; but she differs from most streetcorner prophets in a couple of vital respects. Firstly, with Joan it is always the beginning of the world that is at hand, not the end. Secondly, although much of what she says sounds like nonsense in theory, it has a way of working in practice. In 1945 she formed her own company of actors, Theatre Workshop, in pursuit of a dream of theatre as a place of communal celebration, a Left-wing shrine of Dionysus dedicated to wiping the puritan frown off the popular image of Socialist art. After two decades of toil, the dream is coming to pass. It now seems quite likely that when the annals of the British theatre in the middle years of the twentieth century come to be written, Joan's name will lead all the rest. Others write plays, direct them or act in them: she alone 'makes theatre'.

And, more soberly and historically, Tynan describes her development from the 30s to the 50s:

> The 1930s (which were her teens and twenties) defined her loyalties. She hated those who made profits and befriended those from whose labour profit was made. She wrote film treatments, 'Agitprop' journalism and BBC documen-

taries. Late in that ominous decade she met and married a folk-singer called Ewan MacColl, who managed a theatre group in Manchester and from whom she is now divorced.

'He didn't like the classics,' she says, 'but that didn't matter, because we were always in touch with the *modern* classics – the contemporary, international plays that the commercial blokes ignored. We knew all about Bertolt Brecht in the thirties. On Broadway and Shaftesbury Avenue he's still a novelty in the sixties. Ewan and I must have founded about fifty revolutionary theatre groups in the north before the war. The feeling was always international. You'd go to a mining village in Yorkshire, and there would be three Poles in top hats performing for the workers.'

When Stalin signed his pact with Hitler in 1939, Joan was frozen out of the BBC, and was not readmitted until the Nazis invaded Russia two years later. Throughout the war she was gathering around herself a nucleus of like-thinking actors, and in 1945 she gave them a name: Theatre Workshop.

Their immediate aim was to be a Leftish living newspaper, presenting instant dramatisations of contemporary history. Ewan MacColl wrote many of the scripts, and the troupe's finances were supervised by Gerry Raffles, whom Joan had met in the late 1930s, when he was a burly schoolboy at Manchester Grammar School. The company was run on a completely egalitarian basis: actors, directors, designers and stage staff all got an equal share of the takings. The classics began to seep into the repertoire,* especially those which could be tilted to the Left without undue strain – plays like Lope de Vega's *Fuente ovejuna*, Marlowe's *Edward II* and Jonson's *Volpone*. Theatre Workshop spent eight penniless years on the road, touring Germany, Norway, Sweden and Czechoslovakia as well as Britain, before coming to rest in 1953 at the Theatre Royal, Stratford-atte-Bowe, a shapely Victorian playhouse deep in East London. Here Joan's actors toiled and fasted,

---

* This is not historically accurate: Joan had been directing the classics as part of her repertoire since at least 1936.

many of them so poor that they slept in hammocks slung across the boxes and dressing rooms.

From the mid-50s to the early 60s, she and her company created theatre with an astonishing variety, with tremendous popular appeal, and ultimately with such great commercial success that it destroyed itself. Productions like Behan's *The Quare Fellow* and *The Hostage*, Shelagh Delaney's *A Taste of Honey*, and *Sparrers Can't Sing, Fings Ain't Wot They Used to Be*, and *Oh What a Lovely War* crashed and exploded on to the stages at Stratford, and left audiences reeling with delight and great joy, and young writers and directors breathless with the possibilities of our theatre.

By some strange chance I happened to be at the dress rehearsal of *The Hostage*, with Brendan Behan shouting friendly drunken abuse at the actors through the second half, and them giving him back as good as they got, and Joan charging around muttering, unable to sit still for very long. What was happening on the stage, in the pub down Angel Lane, in the street outside the door, all seemed to be of a piece in the same universe. This group of people were telling a story – they were mediating contemporary reality, but in a way that the Royal Court or the West End or the repertory theatres had not dreamt of: they were telling it the way the working class saw it, and in a way that the working class could enjoy, and, what is more, *did* enjoy.

There is a moral tale going round, which Tynan falls victim to, which says that the working class rejected Joan Littlewood's work, that her theatre was full of trendies from the West End. Now while it is true that in the mid-50s the Theatre Royal was *not* crowded with merry Cockneys, and that Rolls-Royces *were* to be seen outside the door – mostly those of West End managers come to rip off the show – this is not the whole story. Their work touring round the Manchester area gave her, and her company, a real basis for creating theatre for popular audiences. In Scotland people still come up to me after 7:84 Scotland shows and talk with clear and fond memories of 'the Ewan MacColl shows' during the late forties. I am told they were *very* well-attended, and I imagine there were very few Rolls-Royces outside the door. No, Joan and the company who worked with her had worked hard and learnt the cruel way about entertaining the working class before Brendan Behan blew in with his wonderful piles of paper – his laughs and songs and his sentiment and his rebelliousness – with his exploration of, and illumination of the life of Dublin. Avis Bunnage, who first played the mother in *A Taste of Honey*, had toured with Theatre Workshop for years before Shelagh Delaney appeared with the play – and Avis was able to get to work with Joan on that part in a way that brilliantly conned the audience up to the point where they realized they were being conned, then fell apart to reveal another whole layer of human being underneath. Ken Tynan complained that he couldn't understand why the mother kept delivering her lines to the audience! Not only was she the kind of woman who buttonholed every passing person, but also that *kind* of woman was the basis of a whole line of Lancashire comic ladies – ending up with Hilda Baker – who played the variety halls, the pantos, the summer seasons and the clubs. The way Joan directed that character came straight from that line.

David Edgar, in his laconic dismissal of an entire cultural tradition quoted earlier, says: 'it is interesting that they [some groups and companies] have achieved most when they have employed forms actually peripheral to the urban British working class. Joan Littlewood's *Oh What a Lovely War*, for example, used the Pierrot show (a basically Italian form, translated into British seaside entertainment).' Now there are many things to be said about this. First, the Pierrot show at the seaside in the 20s and 30s was a totally British working-class form, well-known and loved by the mums and dads of the 1950s. Secondly, the style of presentation, the construction, the relationship between those actors and the audience, the way of singing the war songs, the degree of sentiment and the mix-in of comedy in some of the cameos, all these and much more, owed everything to music-hall, variety and ENSA-show forms, not one of them 'peripheral to the urban working class'. And the urban working class came to see the show, and loved it.

What was striking about the show was the way Joan and the company had worked together with great confidence in a style that had developed from these popular forms, and were able to use them and the language they created to go beyond a mere imitation of a Pierrot show, or a collection of variety tricks. Because the subject of the show, the unspeakable waste of so many human lives to help the ruling classes of Europe to settle a quarrel over exploiting and killing even more human beings – this subject would exert an immense pressure on *whatever* form were to be employed. In this instance, it forced Joan and the company to create an immensely powerful piece of theatre. If you want to see how to make a disgusting mess of the same material, go and see Richard Attenborough's film of the same name. See what some truly bourgeois confusion, and a great deal of American money, can do to destroy something strong and valuable.

But *Oh What a Lovely War* had an extraordinary effect on British theatre. In the 60s it was performed and loved in almost every repertory in the country. A new generation of young actors played in it, sang the songs, and heard how Joan's actors had worked on it. The fame of

Theatre Workshop spread, and with it a whole set of attitudes to making theatre. Here are some of Joan's legacies:

1. The feeling in some young directors that *they* were
    capable of conjuring up theatre out of thin air with a
    strong theme and a few actors who could entertain.
2. The feeling in some actors that they could con-
    tribute to the making of the play.
3. The feeling in some theatre organizations that given
    the right director, actors and theme, they could
    create a house-style that would pull in a working-
    class audience.

All of which brings me to the Liverpool Everyman in
1970. As the 1944 Education Act continued to cause
growing numbers of working-class youths to blunder on
into higher education, some into universities, some even
to Oxford and Cambridge, so more of them came out of
this process, excited by theatre, wanting to be theatre
directors. And of these, a very small number felt, instinc-
tively, that Joan was doing something they wanted to try
to do. And so, almost any number being greater than *one*,
a spreading, a diaspora of Joan's disciples took place
through the theatres. While Tynan and Joan herself were
lamenting and bewailing the destruction of her company
by the acquisition of her shows for the West End, thus
removing an entire company for a year or two so that she
had to start building up yet another company which in
turn could be plundered – while they were lamenting,
Peter Cheeseman was away in Stoke-on-Trent moving a
few actors into a disused cinema and setting out to do
'documentary' plays about the people in the area. Those
that I have seen have owed a great deal to *Oh What a
Lovely War*. Theatre In Education companies, with no
writers and no plays, sprang up and started putting shows
together using a lot of Joan's techniques. Actors coming
out of drama school began to realise it would be a help if

they could sing.

I should like now to trace a personal, verging on the megalomaniac, sequence of events. Some time in 1968 or –9 I was in Liverpool staying with my family. A friend was coming up from London to see a new play at the Everyman theatre, so I said I'd be interested to go along as well, as I'd heard about this place but not been there. I arrived in Hope Street, and we went into this ex-cinema, ex-church hall, and sat with a very few people and watched a highly pretentious piece of avant-garde whimsy, the hero of which was a pair of Siamese twins dressed in green and purple satin. By the interval I could bear it no longer: I asked my friend if she had in fact been to Liverpool before, to which she replied that she had, but only to sit in theatres and watch other equally awful plays. I suggested that a trip to stand and stare at the dock wall might prove more entertaining, and she, being a metropolitan lady of the theatre, agreed with a certain amount of caution. We escaped from the Everyman, and I vowed never to return. I was shocked, and appalled, that a second theatre in Liverpool should be created merely to extend the whimsical experimental department of cosmopolitan bourgeois high culture. This was, after all, Liverpool, where the dialogue in the street is matched only in Dublin, and where the Liverpool poets were already dragging in large audiences for their poetry readings.

However, there it was, and what could be done about it? About a year later, in autum 69, I was back in Liverpool, and noticed that the Everyman was doing a play about Bessie Braddock, the famous, or infamous, or anyway large Labour MP and personality of the 40s and 50s. This seemed a bit more to the point, and at least something to do with Liverpool. I broke my vow and went. I found that a new director had taken over, a man from Hull with a degree in Drama from Bristol University called Alan Dossor: he had an immense admiration for Joan Littlewood, had studied her work and her audiences, had done some time with Peter Cheeseman at Stoke, and started directing at Nottingham Playhouse under John Neville. He had assembled a company of excellent young actors, who worked in the inventive, confident, audience-grabbing way of Theatre Workshop, and the story was told with a certain amount of pace and variety. There was not much music, however, and the writing was not very sharp in the way Scouse can be. However, in subject, style and attack, Alan was obviously going somewhere positive. I met him, and decided to try to work with him to fill this theatre: the Braddock show was playing to only 30 per cent, a hangover from the Siamese twins era – I felt this was wrong.

The first thing I wrote for them was a group of five short plays called *Unruly Elements*. Four of them were set in Liverpool, and were mostly comic, linked by a series of authoritarian figures talking semi-comprehensible gibberish to the audience. The sets of each play were different, but the permanent framework was a group of standing or hanging giant blown-up objects, like a four-foot toothbrush or a six-foot-high packet of cigarettes.

The audience figures went up to 75 per cent, and the audience responded to the jokes, the presence of recognizable local people and problems on the stage, and the style of the pieces, which varied a little, but which was on the whole full of verbal attack, not at all naturalistic in its pacing, articulateness, or compression. The plays, and the actors and director, created a sense of excitement about the theatre within the community; and encouraged by a determined publicity campaign, by the price of the tickets, by the informality, lack of middle-class bullshit about the theatre, and by the fact that you could get a decent pint of ale before, during and after the show, some

young working-class blokes came with their wives for a
night out. They enjoyed themselves and sent their
friends. As the theatre is near the university, quite a few
students from there and the Poly began to take an interest. Oddly enough, very few of the regular 'theatre
goers' of Liverpool ever came: they had the Playhouse in
the centre of town with the West End, and occasional
Royal Court plays to go and see. The way was open to a
new kind of theatre.

After *Unruly Elements*, Alan tried to mount a show
based on Brecht's *The Private Life of the Master Race*,
with several writers contributing short scenes about contemporary living. It was interesting in that a whole
jumble of styles emerged from the writers, and we could
see what was working with the audience, and guess why.
But all the time I was quite sure that the thing to do was to
fill the theatre, and I knew that then we could really
move, and take the audience with us.

The rock concert is one form of entertainment that had
fascinated me, partly because I like a lot of that kind of
music, partly because the Beatles, Loving Spoonful and
the folk-rock groups had developed lyrics which were
literate and worth listening to, and partly because the
UFO groups like Pink Floyd had established a whole
rather twee performance, or acting level, during and
between their numbers. Alan Dossor asked me to write
another show, and I suggested a musical in the form of a
rock concert, with the actors performing a story and a
band performing a series of numbers, the whole set in
Liverpool, with the central story involving a Liverpool
girl who goes to university and feels she is leaving her
class behind, and the working-class boyfriend who
couldn't make it to university, but who gets off with a
cute middle-class girl he meets while driving his delivery
van. And their mums and dads. We found a local band –
ex-folk, gone electric, now playing heavy beat in a disco

in Seacombe and hating it – who were delighted to come in and write the tunes and perform.

Needless to say, this simple form-concept developed in the writing. The whole thing started off with the two dads in 1940, fire-watching over Liverpool during the blitz, singing Flanagan and Allen numbers, then having a horrifying vision of their children and even worse themselves in the future – thirty years ahead. But this served to introduce another sequence of popular songs, and to give an overview from time to time; the main action went on loosely in the shape of a rock concert, with scenes.

What was really interesting and exciting was that this was one of the most successful shows ever on Merseyside. The working class, young and old, flocked to the Everyman. We played to 109 per cent of capacity, which is really quite full, for the three weeks scheduled, and then came back for another three weeks, and could have gone on for another three. That audience did stay. Alan, as director, found ways to present Shakespeare and other new writers, and Brecht, that kept faith with that audience's expectations. Last year, with Chris Bond in charge, the company 'got together' a show called *Love and Kisses from Kirkby* about that massive housing estate and its history – and the theatre was packed from start to finish of the run.

In 1972 I was in the Fisher-Bendix factory while it was being occupied by the workforce. Almost every worker there that I spoke to had been to the Everyman, and was going to keep on going. And the work at the Everyman was getting better, livelier and more like real theatre than anything I had seen at the Royal Court or the Old Vic.

*   *   *

In the next lecture I would like to talk more specifically about the styles, techniques and devices of this kind of theatre. But I'd like to conclude now by discussing some fairly generalized differences between the demands and tastes of bourgeois and of working-class audiences. I first drew up this list, which I consider to be highly contentious, for the week-end conference on political theatre held in Cambridge last year (1980). At that time there was unfortunately no opportunity to discuss these assertions. The first difference is in the area of *directness*. A working-class audience likes to know exactly what you are trying to do or say to it. A middle-class audience prefers obliqueness and innuendo. It likes to feel the superiority of exercising its perceptions which have been so expensively acquired, thus opening up areas of ambiguity and avoiding any stark choice of attitude. In *Lay Off*, for example, a show with the English 7:84, we spoke straight to the audiences about what we thought of the multinationals. In a factory occupation where we played the show at Swinton, just outside Manchester, there was no problem whatsoever. It was appreciated that we said what we thought. Equally in Murray Hall in East Kilbride there was no problem. But after a performance in London in Unity Theatre, a socialist publisher came up to me and said, 'I don't like to be told what to think, I preferred *Fish in the Sea*.' Now the national press who saw the show felt patronized, but not the working class of Manchester because they knew we were saying what we thought and they were prepared to weigh it up. Some critics even said they thought we were patronizing the working class; but in fact, they were, because the working-class audiences have minds of their own and they like to hear what your mind is.

Second, *comedy*. Working-class audiences like laughs; middle-class audiences in the theatre tend to think laughter makes the play less serious. On comedy working-class audiences are rather more sophisticated. Many working-class people spend a lot of their lives making jokes about themselves and their bosses and their world as it changes.

So the jokes that a working-class audience likes have to be good ones, not old ones; they require a higher level of comic skill. Comedy has to be sharper, more perceptive, and more deeply related to their lives. The Royal Court audience, for example, doesn't laugh very much, and most comedy in the West End is mechanical or weak; in a club, it is vital to have good jokes and sharp comedy. The nature of much working-class comedy is sexist, racist, even anti-working class. We all know the jokes about big tits and pakis and paddies and the dockers and the strikers – there are millions of jokes current in these areas. Therefore, without being pompous about it, comedy has to be critically assessed. The bourgeois comedy, largely of manners, or of intellect, tends to assume there is a correct way of doing things and that that is the way of the average broadminded commuter or well-fed white, etc. Working-class comedy is more anarchic and more fantastical, the difference between the wit and wisdom of the Duke of Edinburgh and Ken Dodd.

Third, *music*. Working-class audiences like music in shows, live and lively, popular, tuneful and well-played. They like beat sometimes, more than the sound of banks of violins, and they like melody above all. There's a long submerged folk tradition which is still there. It emerged recently as a two million sale for a song called 'Mull of Kintyre'; but standards of performance are demanded in music and many individuals in working-class audiences are highly critical and have high standards about the music in shows. But the music is enjoyable for itself, for emotional release, and for the neatness of expression of a good lyric, or a good tune. Middle-class theatre-goers see the presence of music generally as a threat to the seriousness again, unless of course it is opera, when it's different. Big musicals, lush sounds and cute tunes are O.K. in their place, but to convey the emotional heart of a genuine situation in a pop song is alien to most National Theatre goers. Music is there for a bit of a romp to make it a jolly evening.

(4) Fourth, *emotion*. In my experience a working-class audience is more open to emotion on the stage than a middle-class audience who get embarrassed by it. The critics label emotion on stage mawkish, sentimental, etc. Of course, the working-class audiences can also love sentimentality; – in fact, I quite enjoy a dose of it myself, at the right moment, as does everybody – but emotion is more likely to be apologized for in Bromley than in the Rhondda Valley.

(5) Fifth, *variety*. Most of the traditional forms of working-class entertainment that have grown up seem to possess this element. They seem to be able to switch from a singer to a comedian, to a juggler, to a band, to a chorus number, to a conjurer, to a sing-along, to bingo, to wrestling, to strip-tease, and then back again to a singer, and a comedian and a grand 'Altogether' finale, with great ease. If we look at music-hall, variety theatre, club entertainment, the *ceilidh* in Scotland, the *noson llawen* in Wales, panto, and through to the Morecambe and Wise show on television, you can see what I'm talking about.

The middle-class theatre seems to have lost this tradition of variety round about 1630, when it lost the working class and it has never rediscovered it. The now-dominant strain in British middle-class theatre can be traced back to Ibsen by way of Shaw and Rattigan, and so on. The tradition is one of two or three long acts of concentrated spoken drama, usually with no more than five or six main characters. The actors communicate the plot by total immersion in the character they are playing, and move around on a set or sets made to look as much like the real thing as possible. The variety within this kind of theatre is more a question of variation of pace and intensity while doing essentially the same thing throughout. I make no value judgements on these formal elements, merely note that the bourgeois is no less bizarre in its essence than the popular, and one might be forgiven for seeing more creative possibilities in the latter. However, the received opinion is that the former is more serious, and is more capable of high art.

Six, *effect.* Working-class audiences demand more ⑥ moment-by-moment effect from their entertainers. If an act is not good enough they let it be known, and if it's boring they chat amongst themselves until it gets less boring, or they leave, or they throw things. They like clear, worked-for results: laughs, respectful silence, rapt attention to a song, tears, thunderous applause. Middle-class audiences have been trained to sit still in the theatre for long periods, without talking, and bear with a slow build-up to great dramatic moments, or slow build-ups to nothing at all, as the case may be. Through TV, radio and records, working-class audiences have come to expect a high standard of success in achieving effects. They know it comes from skill and hard work, and they expect hard work and skill.

Seven, *immediacy.* This is more open to argument, ⑦ even more so than what I have stated so far. But my experience of working-class entertainment is that it is in subject matter much closer to the audience's lives and experiences than, say, plays at the Royal Shakespeare Company are to their middle-class audiences. Of course there is a vast corpus of escapist art provided for the working class; but the meat of a good comic is the audience's life and experience, from Will Fyffe to Billy Connolly, or from Tommy Handley to Ken Dodd. Certainly in clubs, pantos and variety shows this is the material that goes down best. A middle-class audience can be more speculative, metaphysical, often preferring the subject to

be at arm's length from their daily experience. It prefers
paradigms or elaborate images to immediacy, an interesting parallel from *Timon of Athens* to, for example, a
comedy directly about the decline of the private sector.

Eight, *localism*. Of course, through television,
working-class audiences have come to expect stuff about
Cockneys, or Geordies, or Liver birds, and have become
polyglot in a way not very likely some years ago. But the
best response among working-class audiences comes
from characters and events with a local feel. Middle-class
audiences have a great claim to cosmopolitanism, the
bourgeoisie does have a certain internationality, inter-
changeability. I can't imagine Liverpool Playhouse
crowds reacting very differently from, say, Leeds Playhouse, or Royal Lyceum, Edinburgh, audiences to the
latest Alan Ayckbourn comedy. They all receive it,
anyway. Just as they all get imitations of the National
Theatre and the Royal Shakespeare's 'Aldwych's greatest
hits'. Yet this bourgeois internationality must be distinguished from internationalism, which is an ideological
attribute that ebbs and flows in the working class alarm-
ingly, but which can be there.

Nine, *localism*, not only of material, but also a *sense of
identity* with the performer, as mentioned before. Even if
coming from outside the locality, there is a sense not of
knowing his or her soul, but a sense that he or she cares
enough about being in that place with that audience and
actually knows something about them. Hence the huge
success of Billy Connolly in Glasgow, of Max Boyce in
South Wales. Working-men's clubs in the north of
England depend on this sense of locality, of identity, of
cultural identity with the audience. There are few
middle-class audiences who know or care where John
Gielgud, for example, came from. They don't mind if he
is a bit disdainful when he's in Bradford, because he's a

great man, an artist, and he exists on another planet.

There are many other broad general differences but these are enough to indicate that if a socialist theatre company is interested in contacting working-class audiences with some entertainment, they can't simply walk in with a critical production of Schiller, or even a play written and performed in a style designed to appeal to the bourgeoisie of Bromley, or even the intelligentsia of NW1. A masterpiece might survive, of course. I'm not saying that the working class are incapable of appreciating great art in the bourgeois tradition. They may well be, but if a theatre company wants to speak to the working class, it would do well to learn something of its language, and not assume that the language of bourgeois theatre of the twentieth century is all that is worthy of being expressed.

There is a danger that in schematically drawing up a list of some features of working-class entertainment I am indulging in what is called 'tailism', i.e. trailing along behind the tastes of the working class, debased as they are by capitalism; and merely translating an otherwise bourgeois message into this inferior language. It is a real danger and I have seen people with the best intentions falling into it. But this is not the present case for two important reasons. One is, as I have already said, that these features of working-class entertainment must be handled critically. To enumerate once more: directness can lead to simplification; comedy can be racist, sexist, even anti-working class; music can become mindlessness; emotion can become manipulative and can obscure judgement; variety can lead to disintegration of meaning and pettiness; effect for effect's sake can lead to trivialization; immediacy and localism can close the mind to the rest of the world, lead to chauvinism, and 'Here's tae-us-wha's-like-us'-ism; and a sense of identity with the performer can lead to nauseating, ingratiating performances with neither dignity nor perspective.

The second reason is this. Given a critical attitude to these features of working-class entertainment, they contain within them the seeds of a revitalized, new kind of theatre, capable of expressing the richness and complexity of working-class life today, and not only working-class life. In terms of theatre they are some of the first sounds in a new language of theatre that can never be fully articulate until socialism is created in this country. But before then we can work to extend those first sounds into something like speech by making more and more demands of them, by attempting bolder projects with them, and above all, by learning from our audiences whether we are doing it right or not.

4

Theatre Has Begun
to Take Place

In the first lecture I discussed something of the nature of
the dominant bourgeois form of theatre as found at the
Royal Court from 1956 to 1972/3, currently at the
Aldwych, National, the reps, on TV when the word
'prestige' is in the air, and even on film, at the Royal
Opera House, Covent Garden, and running all this week
at the ADC. The following lecture plunged us into darker
Manchester for a totally opposite kind of entertainment,
to see that there *is*, even now, even in England, an identi-
fiably 'working class' culture which is simply *different*
from that bourgeois culture emanating from Sir Peter
Hall's emporium. It speaks a different language. In the
last lecture we saw that there has been for some years a
tradition within British theatre which is fairly coherent
and very active, which began to develop elements of the
forms of working-class entertainment into a new theatrical tradition that identified its work with the interests of
the working class, and sought the working class as its
audience. In this context we looked briefly at the work of
Joan Littlewood and her collaborators in Theatre Workshop, at Peter Cheeseman's work in Stoke-on-Trent, and
in a little more detail at the Liverpool Everyman Theatre.
I differentiated this kind of theatre, involving itself with

working-class audiences and forms, from 'political' theatre which is on the side of the workers but expresses itself in the language of high cultural theatre – important and excellent though that may be. The work of Brecht and Piscator in the 20s is the best example of this genre; they have had many followers from the American Guild Theatre in the 30s down to Brenton and Hare today.

All this really brings us, halfway through these lectures, to the point where we are more or less forced to face the present situation, and to ask ourselves: what are the ways forward for the theatre? Given the solipsistic nature of the dominant mode, and the fact that the writers who provide its most stimulating moments are on the whole utterly opposed to almost everything it stands for, and given, in my case, an overwhelming sensation of nausea in the presence of this kind of theatrical event, the way forward would seem to me to be towards a new kind of theatre developed from popular forms. Over the last ten years I have indeed been involved in many different approaches to this new kind of theatre, and in the final three lectures I propose to raise some of the problems, theoretical and practical, that are to be met with on this way forward. It would be useful now to look in more detail at the way forms of popular culture can both retain their vitality and relationship with a mass audience, *and* work within a more complex theatrical construct; and I should like to extend the idea of form to include ways of performing and relating to audiences, particularly as I've asked Elizabeth MacLennan, one of 7:84's founder-members, to come along. She has a vast experience of the problems, not only of helping to build a play in this way, but also of performing them to many and varied audiences.

But first a word about what is called 'popular' culture. We have seen that David Edgar has dismissed it as 'atrophied' – a word one might more readily have applied to bourgeois culture, given a bleak half-hour with *Time Out*'s West End theatre listings, but it is a common enough attitude. I believe it is an attitude that comes from a profound but automatic élitism, and is usually coupled with ignorance of the complexity of the nature of popular culture, and lack of experience of it. More important, it is a totally undialectical approach to social experience. Let us turn instead to Brecht, who has expressed well the approach to popular culture which will be most fruitful. I quote from his polemic against Lukács, written in exile in 1938:

> Let us recall that the people were for long held back from any full development by powerful institutions, artificially and forcefully gagged by conventions, and that the concept *popular* was given an ahistorical, static, undevelopmental stamp. We are not concerned with the concept in this form – or rather, we have to combat it.
>
> Our concept of what is popular refers to a people who not only play a full part in historical development but actively usurp it, force its pace, determine its direction. We have a people in mind who make history, change the world and themselves. We have in mind a fighting people and therefore an aggressive concept of what is *popular*.
>
> Popular means: intelligible to the broad masses, adopting and enriching their forms of expression/assuming their standpoint, confirming and correcting it/representing the most progressive section of the people so that it can assume leadership, and therefore intelligible to other sections of the people as well/relating to traditions and developing them/communicating to that portion of the people which strives for leadership the achievements of the section that at present rules the nation.

Now in 1938 the German people were in a slightly worse state than the British people today; but Brecht did not, even in exile, write that their culture was 'atrophied'. He grasped the contradictions in German society, he related them to the potential of the people, and of their culture, and even in 1938 he could see a way towards a future.

Similarly, Gramsci, writing in Mussolini's prisons in the 20s and 30s, produced the concept of the 'national popular', again defined largely by its absence. In nineteenth-century Italy, however, the conditions for its existence – not realized – seemed to Gramsci to be:

1. a radical, Jacobin-type political hegemony
2. a national intelligentsia as opposed to a provincial grouping
3. a closeness between intellectuals and people
4. the presence of advanced ideologies, whether bourgeois or socialist.

Now here Gramsci is taking the concept of 'popular culture' and seeing it not as the inert object of sociological description, but as the site of a political struggle. And that, I suggest, is precisely how we should see that concept – indeed, how we engage ourselves with that reality.

"popular" is site of political struggle

And in case I have given the impression that we are doomed to failure let me invoke the music of Kurt Weill, and the music of Theodorakis in Greece, and of Victor Jara in Chile, music which in its specific development from the popular culture challenged the hegemony of bourgeois culture, became symbolic of the people's voice and struggle, and which attained at times great heights of artistic achievement. The achievement of this music is what we are talking about. It has its difficulties. I don't need to remind you that Weill was driven into exile, Theodorakis imprisoned many times, most recently in a concentration camp by the Greek junta, and Victor Jara was brutally murdered by Pinochet's men in Santiago. The music of all three was banned in their own country, and Jara's still is. But it exists, and is sung. In the theatre, we have mentioned the Blue Blouse movement in Russia in the 20s, Theatre Workshop in the 50s, and Stoke and Liverpool in the 60s and 70s in Britain. To these we could add the work of Dario Fò in Italy, of Ariane Mnouchkine's Théâtre du Soleil, and no doubt other lesser-known groups in France, the Werktheater in Holland, the many political groups in Sweden, and, for the last ten years, the work of 7:84 Theatre Company in England and Scotland, and the other groups which now work all over Britain in this area, like Belt and Braces, Monstrous Regiment, North-West Spanner, Broadside, Red Ladder – not to mention the innumerable Theatre In Education companies who now also perform outside school time; or the many small companies growing out of the side of the repertory theatres who now do 'community work', like the Glasgow Citizens Group, Theatre Around Glasgow, who tour community centres, halls and clubs round Glasgow, or Borderline, who travel round Ayrshire, or even Tie-up, the Inverness theatre's group, or local groups like Fir Clish, 'the Northern Lights', who travel round the Outer Hebrides performing new work in Gaelic. Many of these groups are related, in personnel or in style, to 7:84 England or 7:84 Scotland. It may well be that none of them, including 7:84, has yet produced a major drama – this we don't know. But there can be no doubt that they constitute a major element in British theatre, with several publishers starting to publish their work, large amounts of money granted by the Arts Councils, and growing audiences all over Britain. Young theatre workers on coming into the theatre are now faced with a choice, and the more enterprising and progressive are going, at least for a time, into the more difficult country of this kind of theatre: it is to this area, rather than to the close-carpeted blandness of the National Theatre's product-range, that we must look for the excitements and achievements of the future.

*   *   *

So, armed with a critical, dialectical approach to popular culture and its forms, with an intimate, if critical, knowledge of the audience, with boundless energy and imagination, and with the kind of political perspective that I outlined in the second of these lectures, what do we do? Well, first of all, we try to find a lot more people with similar attitudes, energy and knowledge, who can bring with them the specific skills needed to create the theatrical event. Skills are needed in writing, directing, composing and making music, acting, singing, moving, choreography, set and costume design, construction and painting, lighting and general electrics, sound engineering, stage management, driving, in administration, publicity and maintaining contacts within the working-class movement and within the theatre and with local authority organizations. Some people may combine several of these skills, but to work efficiently each one of them has to be performed not only with a command of the traditional methods, but also with a critical and creative attitude to those methods when put to serving new purposes. On its simplest level, this means that the designer is shown not the dimensions of a stage, but the dimensions of the inside of a truck. At its most complex, it means, for example, a total reappraisal of the relationship between the actor, the character he or she is playing, the nature of the relationship with the audience of the specific form employed, the idea of history (and the individual's perception of history), and the idea of theatre as public emblem of a private, shared emotion. These problems of radical reappraisal are the everyday meat and drink of this kind of theatre: life in it can only be a succession of decisive solutions to them, as they present themselves, on *all* levels – and the success or failure of the project depends upon the quality of those decisions, those solutions.

Now clearly there are within any group specific unifying principles which give a certain coherence to these decisions, which relate directly to the values, political, theatrical and personal, of that group, and which must be defined to a great degree by the actual capabilities of the individual members of the group. Therefore in any critical examination of the work of such a theatre or company or group, it will be important to try to establish these unifying principles, and to be aware of the limits to the capabilities of its members. And in any attempt to *create* such a group, it must be realized that these unifying principles have a habit of emerging looking rather different *after* a series of decisions from the way they looked before.

However, the area – and it is only one area – of decision-making that we were going to look at was that of the creative, critical use of working-class forms of entertainment in the making and performing of this kind of theatre. And it's high time we got a bit more specific, so I'd like to take advantage of Elizabeth MacLennan's being here to ask her to read a speech from *Little Red Hen*, a speech by the Old Hen, a character that she created. The story so far is that Old Henrietta, a 75-year-old battling Clydeside socialist who has lived through the great days of the Red Clyde, who supported Jimmy Maxton and worked to get him elected, has come into this theatre in 1975, to find a row of Harry Lauder figures giving an appalling 'light entertainment from Scotland' show, all dressed up in Japanese tartan: one of the troupe is her grand-daughter, Young Henrietta, a fervent Scottish Nationalist, who believes that a new Golden Age of Scottish politics is about to dawn. Old Henrietta enlists the support, unwilling, of the rest of the troupe, to act out for Young Henrietta just where they went wrong in the past, and where she is going even more wrong in the present. After scenes in Westminster, and scenes of the family at home, they eventually come to the defeat of the General Strike and the bitter sense of betrayal felt by many millions of workers at that time. The scene ends with Charlie, her husband, reflecting that they fought, and they lost, and now they are going to pay the price, for years to come. He goes off, and Old Hen, who has been watching Young Hen playing her part in the scene, turns away. Young Hen comes back and joins her and listens as she tells what happened next:

> OLD HEN: Aye, and so we did. Soon Charlie wasnae the only one on the parish – there was thousands and thousands queueing for their dole-money – if they were lucky enough to get any. We got another Labour government alright – aye, Ramsay MacDonald rode again – we put him in to increase the benefit – do you know what he did? He cut it. When he came in, one man in ten was unemployed – in two years, one man in five. Do you know what we had to dae? Ah've seen my ain mother traipse on her two feet frae Bridgeton to Skinners in Sauchiehall Street, wi' a pillow-slip tae fill wi' broken loaves that naebody wanted – and, if she was lucky, squashed meringues. The next day she'd be up to the Bermaline for two pennorth of broken biscuits. First Charlie lost his job, then my father, then my mother – I was still going on fine, nineteen shillings a week frae the sweatshop, stitching up ball-gowns and pin-stripe suits. Made me sick to think of people dressin' up like that wi' other people starvin' near to death in the same city – still, it was keepin' me in work: till then what happened? Just what I needed maist in the world – twins.
>
> YOUNG HEN: You mean my Uncle Freddie in Vancouver?
>
> OLD HEN: Aye, and your Uncle Charlie that was washed away in the floods in Darwin, Australia. Here, did he no' send you a boomerang?

YOUNG HEN: Aye. It didnae work.

OLD HEN: I fed them till they were five months; I was like a rake. I heard you got one and sixpence a week extra frae the parish if you were feeding a wain ... the bastard asked me if I could prove it—I felt like whippin' one out and gie'n him a squirt in the eye. Still, we got by. Mince and tatties on a Thursday and there was aye bone-soup – if you could get a bone that is. It was hard to get a bone ... see Jessie Nolan, her they've stuck in the Eventide Home – well she had this great big knee bone: Here, says I – what kind of a beast did you get that off of, an elephant out of the zoo? Don't let on, says she. Here, I says, gie's a lend of it after you've finished with it. Three pots of soup came out of that bone – it went from her pot tae mine, and then tae May Armstrong up the stair – and that's God's truth.

Ach, the thirties was nae time to be trying to get by, in Glasgow or anywhere else – they *had* to start another war, to get the men some work. And our great parliamentary heroes? What did they do? Most of the Great Reds of the Clyde slid into the Labour Party, in the hope of turnin' into Prime Ministers. Not Jimmy Maxton, no – he became a sad, solitary voice, crying in the wilderness. Nor Wheatley. He died. Still a Pape, but still fightin'. And the TUC? Spineless. And then, to cap it all, doesnae Charlie decide he's going off to Spain to do battle with the Fascists? Oh aye – it was the right courageous thing to dae. But was there no' enough to fight here? I telt him – if anyone's gonnae get shot, it'll be you – but no – he knew. Well, I was proved right by a Fascist bullet, wallop, right between the eyes – he was aye pigheaded. Leaving me wi' three wains to bring up – if I could have got a haud of him, I'd have kicked his heed in.

Poor Charlie; we need a few more like him today.

Now that speech, or should I say the experience of

seeing Liz do that speech to audiences of two to three
hundred in drinking clubs down the Clyde, to five
hundred shipyard workers and their families in Clydebank Town Hall, to riotous packed houses of eight to
nine hundred Glaswegians, mostly working class, in the
Citizens Theatre – that experience brought together
many struggles, with victories and failures, over the previous four years. It was the fruit not just of one piece of
work, but of a developing relationship with an audience.

It had its immediate roots in *The Cheviot, the Stag and
the Black, Black Oil*, which was 7:84 Scotland's first show
and which was immensely popular not only in the Highlands, but also in all the places in the industrial belt where
we had taken it. There is a strong bond between the Highlands and the Clyde, and of course with Edinburgh: the
families of well over half the working class of those areas
settled there *from* the Highlands for precisely the reasons
given in the play. They, the much-maligned industrial
proletariat, responded to the *ceilidh* form with recognition and pleasure. After all, Calum Kennedy had been
dragging in thousands of them to Calum's *ceilidh* in the
Glasgow Pavilion theatre for years, they see *ceilidhs* on the
television, many of them go back to the Highlands on
holiday and take part in impromptu *ceilidhs* in the bar or
in their granny's parlour.

They responded to the Gaelic folk-singing and the
fiddle playing and the folk tunes with no problem, in fact
with great pleasure. There is, and has been for some time,
a massive boom in music loosely termed 'folk', particularly in Scotland. This contributes a tremendous amount
of music from the history of the people to the generally
available pool of cultural experience, music with all kinds
of beauty, expressiveness, meaning and, above all, potential. Rescued from the Victorian drawing-room by A.L
Lloyd, Ewan MacColl and many other singer-

entertainers, popularized by Joan Baez, and developed by many hundreds of talented groups of singers and musicians in Scotland, Ireland, America, Brittany, even in England – certainly much of it is very popular in England – it now makes its way into the record rack of the young car worker, into the repertoire of the pub singer. The biggest smash hit on the entertainment scene in Scotland is, after all, a folk singer: Billy Connolly. And Scotland's current contribution to the ratings battle on British TV is another ex-folk singer, Isla St Clair. So why should the urban proletariat respond with amazement to Gaelic and other Scots folk music?

They also responded very strongly to the comedy, as you might expect. They appreciated also the directness with which relevant historical facts were presented, and the way we declared our interests, our position, our perspective, and our conclusion. This directness opened up the struggle of the Highlanders to contact with their struggles, in a very real way; for example, it helped to create pressure within the Labour Party from all over Scotland for some measures to reform estate-ownership and land use in the Highlands. The reception of *The Cheviot* in the industrial areas indicated many things about our future work.

The Cheviot, popular and appreciated as it was, did not touch on the urban misery, the architectural degradation, the raw, alcohol-riddled despair, the petty criminal furtiveness, the bleak violence of living in many parts of industrial Scotland. Nor had we performed *The Cheviot* in the miners' clubs, Trades Council clubs, the union halls of central Scotland. We resolved to do both with the show we mounted after *The Cheviot*, called *The Game's a Bogey*. The title is a Glasgow children's phrase meaning the game's up, or over, or spoilt. In a narrow way it was used with reference to the alternation of Wilson and Heath at

that time, the pointless two-party system in which the
objects were always the working people; but in a more
general way it referred to the state of the lives of many
people in our audience. Against these were set the life and
words of John Maclean, pioneer Scottish socialist activist
and teacher of Marxist economics to many thousands of
workers in Scotland in the first twenty years of this
century. In some ways that is quite a sophisticated operation, theatrically coping with switches from 1907 to 1973
and then back to 1913, and so forth; historically sophisticated in coping with two periods not in parallel but in
ironical distantiation, and politically sophisticated in relating Maclean's words to their historical context, but
pointing them, by way of their defeat at that time,
through to the consequences of their non-fulfilment
today. Anyway, that is something of what we set out to
achieve.

I think in many ways it would be better to describe the
realization of the show as an event rather than analysing
the text on the page, and the performance that will always
stay in my mind was that in the Glenrothes CISWO*
Club. Glenrothes is a New Town in Fife, sitting on an old
coalfield. In the middle of the new town, a large glass and
concrete building looking like a small light industrial
advance factory. Inside, an upstairs bar where members
get beer subsidized by the Coal Board, even if they've
never been near a pit, and downstairs, at the back, the
clubroom, a huge concrete barn with a bar all down one
side, tables and chairs for three hundred, a smallish but
high stage at one end, and a tiny dressing room behind it.
Tickets had been sold at 20p each to members and 50p
each to non-members: about 220 had gone in advance.
The fame of *The Cheviot* had helped to sell some, others
had been press-ganged by our supporters in Glenrothes,

* Coal Industry Social and Welfare Organization.

others came to see what it was.

We set the show up as well as we could on the stage, and rigged the sound equipment and lighting, and arranged the tables so there was some chance of being seen from the far end, and tried to relay speakers so that we might be heard as well. We put away a Chinese carry-out and a few subsidized pints as the hall began to fill. The bar in the hall, like all busy bars, was making a hell of a noise and a lot of money. The club officials were against our putting any of their lights out at all, but this would have made our lighting plot more than ineffective. A compromise was reached. The noise in the hall was heavy – and boozy. It occurred to all of us that the club would make more money if we *didn't* perform and the audience could concentrate on serious drinking for the evening. But no – we were going to go on: to the end, if we had done our work properly.

The reason I remember Glenrothes so clearly is that it was the very first miners' club we had ever played in, and the very first time we performed *The Game's a Bogey* to an audience in that situation. I was literally terrified: the consequences of failure to please would be direct and painful; the consequences of pleasing but failing to communicate would be indirect but even more painful in the long run. The company were also terrified, but heroic.

On came the band, all acting as well as musical members of the company, in matching red blazers with 7:84 on the pocket. Nobody paid any attention, and as they launched into the instrumental opening, the noise level got higher as people yelled to be heard above the band. On bounced Bill Paterson to do his compère job, off went some of the lights, and up came our lights and follow-spot. As Bill chatted breezily to the audience and introduced, with gags, the members of the band, the general noise level was still high, and the bar very busy

and very loud. It was really only when Terry Neason
came on, burst into her verses of the opening song, and
blatantly vamped them, that something approaching
attention was established. The show, ultimately, had a
certain amount to say about sexism, but I regret to say
that it was in some measure for sexist reasons that we
established contact with the members of the Glenrothes
CISWO Club. This, plus the fact that she has a good
raunchy sort of voice, plus the fact that the whole tempo
of the number picked up when she came on, and the band
suddenly were able to perform with some attack, all
helped to turn a few heads, even those at the bar, towards
the stage. The number ends with a big bang, and as a few
claps broke out, suddenly police sirens, blue lights flash-
ing, general scramble to get off the stage, and a Goon
Show policeman appears running in to the hall – he is
about seven feet tall, with an enormously long overcoat, a
trilby stuffed on top of his helmet to indicate that he is
incognito, a false chin (with a false pluke) to cover the
straggling red beard of our fiddler, and a false accent and
false height to throw his enemies into confusion. He runs
and leaps onto the stage, driving away the hooligans of
the band, then informs the audience that he is Lachlan
MacDonald, in search of Red trouble-makers, particularly one John Maclean, who is stirring up industrial
strife among the peace-loving workers of Scotland. He
goes off threatening to kill them, smash them, etc.
because he hates violence: police sirens sound. Now the
audience really are intrigued. His acting of 'Kill them!
Smash them!' is strong, and even though contained in a
joke, still commands attention. As he goes, the company
come back on and tell the startled audience that there
really was a Lachlan MacDonald, who really *did* go round
trailing John Maclean – and they tell them who this John
Maclean was. Bill Paterson, as he adds his bit of infor-

mation, is putting on the coat and hat of Maclean; he then delivers a reconstruction of a shortish Maclean speech. The audience are now confronted with the history and the politics: they become more interested, rather than less. But we have an unwritten entertainment contract established at the beginning of the show. Lachlan again comes on, and arrests Maclean with a few awful knock-knock jokes, and takes him off, ordering the company to get on with the fun-loving Scottish variety show. Another number ('Let's take a walk down by the Clyde') is the response, a catchy, poppy number, but describing life in the high-rise cardboard cartons that sway from side to side by the silvery Clyde: a nice number, and a few laughs. Then on comes our first modern character, Ina, a young girl of eighteen going out to the dance. She bursts on to do a stand-up comic routine, with terrible jokes about pan-stick and polyfilla, but she gets the audience interested in the character she's playing, just like Buttons in the panto. Then she settles down to dream about Mr Right as she reads her teen-magazine, and Terry and the band perform, for her and the audience, a song about her situation and her dreams, and the fantasy factory: it's a gentle, folk-rock tune that develops with urgency and anger into the section about the lies she is being sold about men and her future. By now, the audience are sitting, taking it in. Theatre has begun to take place.

I shan't go on with this story – I hate it when I'm told the plots of plays – but I wanted to give you those few minutes in some detail for several reasons. First of all, to show the perils of plunging into drinking clubs with *any* kind of entertainment, let alone something with pretensions to being theatre. The working class has been told for so long that theatre is not for their likes, has been so put off by the middle-class's appropriation of theatre, indeed of all art, that it resents, at least heavily distrusts, the whole idea. It expects the language of the whole experience of theatre to be rebarbative with class content, and to be aimed at insulting itself and its families, at best by patronising, at worst by spreading slanderous lies. Little wonder the class needs reassurance, at least to begin with. Once this thing called theatre has been reappropriated by the working class, it will begin to respond in a lively, intelligent and critical way. The people will make the direct comparison between what you are showing and their experience of life, and if you are found lacking, then it'll let you know. And it has very high expectations of what you offer because they have been starved of it, and want it, and actually need it as a non-alienating part of their culture, of their lives.

The point about *The Game's a Bogey* is, really, that it took the trouble to contact and reassure the audiences, to show the signs of class solidarity in a theatrical and personal as well as political way, and to speak the language of the audience but in a new and intriguing way. Anyway, that's what it set out to do. The show goes on to introduce two other main characters, a country-and-western singing Hard Man, who meets up with Ina in a dance and soon has to marry her; and a vicious young pre-punk character called McWilliam singing Slade-type stuff about the game he's got to join. We interact between their advancing stories, at work, at home, at the doctor's, in the pub, etc., and the relentless and increasingly nasty pursuit of Maclean by Lachlan, and Maclean's speeches about the situation of the Glasgow working class, and other scarcely plot-related incidents or turns involving Sir Mungo McBungle, a local failed industrialist, his wife Lavinia, who advocates portable gas-ovens for troublemakers and supports Teddy Taylor, and Andy McChuckemup, a fly wee Glasgow wheeler-dealer, who makes a return appearance after his success in *The Cheviot*. Somewhere in amongst it there is a tragedy, not of one person, but of a whole society. It is the tragedy you feel walking round the streets of Govan, of Clydebank, of the Gorbals – of a hope once burning bright, but now gone out: but not for ever.

Now *because* we had taken *The Game's a Bogey* round and built audiences who knew and enjoyed our work, and who trusted us, we were able in the next shows to develop, to push the style in all kinds of directions, to make increasingly complex statements, to invent new devices within the general framework of a style that we knew would work, even to try out bits we weren't sure of: just to see.

The unifying principles of the company were, amongst others, to keep faith with that audience by going back time after time, by working hard to maintain the highest possible standards of entertainment and imagination, in writing and performance, by developing our personal contacts with the audience, listening to their comments and learning from them, by expanding our political and historical work into areas that were important and showing clearly their relationship with the lives of the audience. We tried to 'keep faith' also by changing, by not simply repeating, either in content or form, the first show simply because it was successful, but to keep thinking, moving ahead of the audience's expectations in all areas. They would follow us now more readily than they would some unknown bunch of middle-class actors. They, in fact, had appropriated us: we belonged to them, and when we did not appear for longer than six months, there were complaints.

In fact, the next new show we did in Scotland was a Highland 'Concert Party' show called *Boom*, which did two tours of the North and West, a small industrial-belt tour, then we did a less politically and historically orien-

ted show called *My Pal And Me*, which disappointed
some of our more politically Calvinist supporters but
which certainly played the clubs with a lot of success. In it
the pop concert idea I mentioned last time, in connection
with my early work with Liverpool Everyman, was tried
in a touring situation: I personally felt it was not such a
great success, and in many ways it was a makeshift
arrangement, but it spoke the language, and did the main
part of our job In the next show, *Little Red Hen*, I resolved to go further in all directions and to demand a
great deal more of our audiences theatrically, politically
and historically.

As I said earlier, it kicked off with an outrageous
opening number, starting with one Harry Lauder in
bumbee tartan, soon joined by another ten, all swinging
sickeningly into 'Stop your tickling, Jock'. The style
related to all the forms I have mentioned, with the
extraordinarily identifiable qualities I listed last week –
*directness, comedy, music, emotion, variety, effect, imme-
diacy* to the audience's lives, *localism*, and a sense of identity with the performers, all treated critically,
dialectically and with imagination and skill from the
company. But it did not always use the forms with the
same literalness that we had used in *The Game's a Bogey*,
but more freely, more coherently, with a great deal still of
discontinuity, but more internal coherence and a more
satisfying rhythm through the show.

In this way we came to the point where, having worked
for it in her previous scenes, and having established a relationship with the audience, Liz could just sit on a stool
in a spotlight and give out a speech as vulnerable and as
exposed, as long and as quiet as that, and make it work, in
a real way, in a club that to the first ignorant glance might
appear utterly philistine, part of a debased, commercia-
lized, one-dimensional ersatz culture. That speech, and

the rest of *Little Red Hen*, may not attain literary splendour, but it does show how much is *possible*, and I, and I'm sure Liz, can vouch for how satisfying working in this way can be.

But I think I'd better end with a cautionary quote from Sanchez Vazquez – cautionary to me, that is:

> The artist can only create in response to an inner need to express and communicate – freely, not on account of an external demand. This results in a situation analogous to the one Marx pointed out in his discussion of the hostility of capitalism toward art, when artists create in response to an external need imposed by the law of supply and demand, thus subjecting artistic production to the laws of material production.
>
> When an artist creates because of an external need, in conformity with principles, norms, or rules imposed from above, what had been a movement, a vital force, a conscious and sincere reverence for certain creative principles, becomes a formal, external, and therefore false, loyalty. What was alive becomes congealed, inert; this inertia is what exists, like a deadly virus, in all forms of academicism. . . .
>
> . . . We can only grasp concrete reality by truncating or simplifying a complex and rich totality. Marx considered concrete reality to be the unity of the determinations of an object; but however rich the conceptualization of the concrete might be, it never succeeds in grasping the determinations of reality in all their richness. Some of these determinations must be eliminated in favour of others which are more essential, thus moving from a less to a more profound essence. The result is a concept which reflects with increasing richness and depth the richness and depth of the object itself. The process of knowledge, therefore, goes from one abstraction to another in an upward movement that has no end. But theory must also change because reality itself is in a process of change, and

only by changing, by developing, can it grasp concrete reality with greater faithfulness.

As soon as a theory stops changing, or a particular abstraction is regarded as definitive, or a limited set of determining factors is deemed sufficient to express reality, then theory ceases to have any value; if in spite of this we impose a value on that theory as a guide to action ... we should distinguish between a theory which springs from the movement of reality... and what is nothing more than a normative doctrine or strait-jacket for the creative impulse.

While I would not agree with all his formulations, Vazquez there on the one hand warns against the dangers of decreeing that there is only one way of, say, making theatre – we must be certain that there are many. On the other hand, he gives us a model of the richly complex, multi-determined nature of reality which is what the theatre is always struggling towards recreating. If one of the unifying principles of one's sequences of decisions and solutions – and creations – is to move the theatre closer to recapturing the richness, the complexity and the ceaseless dialectical movement of reality, then I think one is pointing in, if not the only, then at least a good direction.

5

Theatre as Political Forum

In the first three lectures I have talked about theatre as an event, with a complex language involving many aspects of that event beyond the verbal construct as recorded on the page; and I have talked about the class meaning of some elements of that language, particularly the entertainment *forms* used or developed or 'moved-on-from' in the presentation of the piece of theatre. In the last lecture I spoke about the forms and language of the kind of theatre that I have been engaged in, a theatre that draws its audience and its language from the working class and their experience of life and entertainment. But of course there are other areas of work in this kind of theatre which raise immense problems, beyond – though not unconnected with – those of form and language.

First and foremost there is the question of what this kind of theatre is going to be *about*. Or, to put it another way, what are the parameters of intellectual complexity and refinement of sensibility that an author will encounter when writing for an audience in a working-men's club in Chorlton-cum-Hardy? We are talking now about content, but in a way the question relates also quite clearly to the form, as the audience have created the form, and are the arbiters of how far that form may be stretched. And this raises the second large question of how this kind of theatre relates to its audience: does it tail along behind, seeking approval? Or does it express its solidarity with it, afraid to criticize? Or does it plunge way 'ahead' of this audience, hoping one or two brave spirits will follow and form a dazzling vanguard? Clearly what unites these two questions is the political perspective of the company. And this in turn raises the third large problem area: that of how a company working in this kind of theatre should be organized internally, of how different it needs to be from a West End management or a Peter Hall subsidiary, and in what ways? Although these three questions – of content, audience-relationship, and internal organisation – may appear to be quite disparate, they can only be looked at together because their common determining factor is the nature of the political/artistic drive behind the whole project.

Now there is a great deal to be said about the relationship between art and politics, but I think perhaps the most important, and neglected, fact is that the relationship is determined by many concrete historical phenomena, occurring on all kinds of level, so that the relationship *changes*.

There is no point in elaborating a timeless, idealized structure somewhere outside history for this relationship; it has to be fought out on the ground of the facts and talents and potentialities of the present, taking into account the relationship of the present with the past, and with the future. Nor, of course, is there only *one* relationship between art and politics which is 'correct' for any one time. But it is important to realize that every writer who *is* a writer will be in a constant process of redefining that relationship in the context of his or her own experience, skills and talent, and that the quality of his or her work will be profoundly affected by the honesty and rigour of that struggle.

This is most urgent in the theatre. For the theatre is, or can be, the most public, the most clearly political of the art forms. Theatre is the place where the life of a society is shown in public to that society, where that society's assumptions are exhibited and tested, its values are scrutinized, its myths are validated and its traumas become emblems of its reality. Theatre is not about the reaction of *one sensibility* to events external to itself, as poetry tends to be; or the *private* consumption of fantasy or a mediated slice of social reality, as most novels tend to be. It is a public event, and it is about matters of public concern. Now it happens quite frequently that those matters are trivial – in a West End sex-comedy, for example, they are very trivial indeed. But they are presented as matters about which there is a large cultural consensus. They make public, and in a way make political, the sexual attitudes of the mass West End public (at least while they are *being* the mass West End public, if you see what I mean). So even in this rather oblique way, the theatre is by its nature a political forum, or a politicizing medium, rather than a place to experience a rarefied artistic sensibility in an aesthetic void. Theatre launches even the most private thought into a public world, and gives it a social, historical meaning and context as it passes through the eyes and minds of the audience. It is a place of recognition, of evaluation, of judgement. It shows the interaction of human beings and social forces. How could it remove itself from the other public acts of recognition, evaluation and judgement known as politics? How could it ignore the study of past interaction of human beings and social forces known as history? Of course, try as it may, it cannot. What is the more remarkable, then, is that so many theatre writers and critics have repudiated with contempt all the work done in these disciplines of politics and history, and in related areas like social studies, anthropology, psychology, linguistics, etc., as somehow 'inartistic' and therefore boring and unimaginative.

Behind this inarticulate but widespread British grumble there lurks a sentimental, nostalgic image of the romantic poet, a truly dreadful concept of the artistic vision piercing through the gloom of contemporary reality, seizing upon and encapsulating in a few pithy phrases the spirit of our time, all done by 'instinct' or 'inspiration' with no effort of the mind, and all packaged for the convenience of posterity. I'm afraid that's not how it is or, indeed, ever was, particularly with Romantic poets. When Shelley wrote of poets as 'the unacknowledged legislators of the world', he was not complaining about poets being legislators, but noting that they are unacknowledged. His 'Ode to the West Wind' is no less than a call to social revolution, and Shelley's suppressed works, the ones cut from your school selection, are nearly all of a hard-line political nature. Shelley, Byron, Wordsworth, Coleridge, Blake were all men of considerable reading and scientific curiosity, men of intellect. This image of the Romantic poet, this concept of the artist as the inspired amateur with the X-ray imagination, some sort of literary Batman who can leap into a Batmobile transformed from an ordinary Joe into the better half of the dynamic duo whenever he falls to composing plays or verses – this whole line of thinking about contemporary writers is so vulgar, so teeny-bopper in its mindless hero-worshipping, so alienated from reality, that there must be some ulterior motive behind it.

But there it is. Harold Pinter presents an enigmatic face to the camera, writes a play that goes backwards, and he has said something significant, or has – significantly – failed to say something significant. But let John Arden and M. D'Arcy give us an outline of the events leading to an eviction in the west of Ireland, let them include a few relevant historical facts, like the presence of the British army in the north of Ireland, and suddenly Arden has fallen from grace, his 'polemical bigotry' is ruining his art. Perhaps we can begin to detect the ulterior motive: our artists must remain innocent, they must return us from the sour world we know into the Garden of Childhood, where everything is mysterious, with an air of urbanity and sophistication maybe, but always hinting at some unfulfilled promise of unnamed delight. Well, we all know that urge, recognize it, respond to it and even need a bit of it from time to time, but when it is used as a way of keeping the theatre outside the movement of time and intellect, outside the major serious concerns of this century, outside the many-layered struggles of humanity, then this concept of the artist is serving a political purpose, and not one that can long remain hidden, even by Conor Cruise O'Brien, who once knew better. So whether a writer is making a play for a Royal Court or an Achiltibuie audience, he or she must, in my opinion, see every event in the story as determined by many, many forces on many levels; and to present that event in its richness and complexity, he or she must not shrink from introducing as many levels as possible or necessary into the fabric of the play, and in dealing with these levels must not hesitate to make use of the critical apparatus appropriate to that level in its most fully-developed state. In other words, don't be more stupid than you have to be – or more backward, or less demanding – simply because the English bourgeois theatre critics, theatre directors, successful actors, and other writers expect you to be.

The trap, of course, is that theatre *has* 'developed' during the twentieth century, but its line of development has remained stunted, childish, retarded beside the extraordinary and exciting developments in almost all other areas of human activity. It has remained unable to cope, technically, with those other developments, and unable to provide its audience with a complete or even an up-to-date image of life, and so has traditionally retained as an audience only the nostalgic sections of the community, or the other sections when they are feeling nostalgic. So Edward Bond, for example, will resort to sub-Brechtian parables when what we want are facts, or Stoppard will conjure amusingly with the surface trivia of positivist philosophy when what we need is a fundamental demolition job, or Pinter can baffle, bemuse and intrigue about the romantic affairs of the rich when we are desperately trying to find clarity and information about the financial affairs of those paid less than £40 per week. It is interesting that it was Joan Littlewood, in *Oh What A Lovely War*, who invented a way of presenting the exact number killed per battle in the 1914–18 war *at the same time* as showing the individual human emotions of those taking part. But even this is only a device, an approximation. If, as Brecht noted, petroleum resists the five-act form, what do nuclear fusion and micro-processors do to the bourgeois comedy? But the theatre today is full of bourgeois comedy, of one kind or another.

I'm not advocating a trendy 'scientific' theatre, so beloved of Futurists and Expressionists and other choral speakers of the 20s. For one further – perhaps the most important – feature of theatre as a form is that its dimensions are essentially those of the human figure, its communication essentially between one group of people and another actually present in the same space. However extensive and complex human activities may be, they still relate to, and have meaning in terms of groups of individual people. And the theatre is the one medium that forces, by its very limitations, that confrontation between an abstraction and a person, between a system and a group of individual people, between social history, or political theory, and the actual life of a man or a woman. The project of theatre should not be to 'humanize' (i.e. *diminish*) the abstraction, or the theory, rather to enlarge them, simultaneously enlarging the concept of the human, in a dialectical manner. But at what point, one must ask, does this stern intellectual project cease to be 'theatre'? I think it is vitally important to understand that in order to begin to write a play today, one needs first to redefine our inheritance from the history of Western civilization. This may well sound like an absurdly pretentious statement, if you happen to have an absurdly pretentious concept of Western civilization. It merely means that you have to question all your assumptions about life and society, and try to find out where they came from, and evaluate them in a new way, according to the demands of your own and your contemporaries' situation. There are hundreds, nay thousands, of scholars beavering away to find, organize and make available the evidence: it is not difficult to consult their work. But I must stress that this questioning of assumptions, this theoretical struggle, is not a *substitute* for theatre, it is both a preliminary to and an active ingredient in the process of creating theatre. Even as a preliminary it has to be undertaken in a way that is coloured by its subsequent route and destination: a contemporary audience, by way of a piece of theatrical entertainment. In the process of making a piece of theatre, this questioning will continue in all areas, even, as we have seen, into that of form, and the processes of recreating the language of the theatre, as well as the areas of research, evaluating material – for inclusion, cutting, or revision – and determining an actor's attitude to a character, which will help create their performance, and be part of that performance. It will extend through into the smallest detail – the

way a laugh should be handled, the size of the poster, relationships with the janitor of a hall. All this may sound
like a terrible burden to carry around into even the inter-
stices of living, and indeed at times it can be. But if it
becomes a stifling, life-destroying burden, either on the
creative processes or on the lives of the company, then
there is something wrong with the theory, because one of
the demands one must make of a useful, theoretical
approach is that it enriches the creative process, and
liberates the imagination of the company. This is not to
say that if you hit a problem you change your theoretical
framework to suit. What it does is posit the primacy of
the creation of theatre, which is a real thing, in a real
world, and a positive element in society, and in one's
practice as a human being.

But there is more than abstract knowledge, scientific
research and political theory on the external side of our
equation. As the world outside our immediate sphere
grows more complex, more dangerous, more hostile and
ultimately irreconcilable with the sense of confidence and
well-being that we need to face the future – any future –
so individuals will retreat from it into domesticity, or
mysticism, or the warm glow of the boozer, or into soft
drugs like marijhuana or television. Once in this condition of retreat, they are bombarded, willy-nilly, by
powerful organizations within the capitalist state with a
version of contemporary reality called 'news'. Inside their
shells, individuals receive images of a world outside, a
series of (at first glance) unrelated images. Then, at
second glance, perhaps related only *objectively* by the
objective relationships within the reality they describe,
but eventually, this series is discernible as a perspective,
as a subjective selection of events, as a mediation of reality
determined by the power structure that supports those
large organizations which in turn support the power

structure. These are also the people – like Ian Trethowan, director-general of the BBC, Brian Cowgill, controller of Thames TV, Bernard Levin, the redundant theatre critic, Conor Cruise O'Brien, pundit and formerly *Observer* editor, J. W. Lambert, ex-arts editor of the *Sunday Times*, Martin Esslin, recently head of drama BBC radio, and many another – who would prefer theatre, and dramatic writing in general, to stay in the Golden Age of childish innocence and fun, perhaps with a touch of menace or cruelty somewhere in it, to avoid charges of gross escapism; the people who have led Dennis Potter from *Vote Vote Vote for Nigel Barton* to nostalgia for domestic events in the 30s, and for rural childhood in the 40s. Martin Esslin has even gone so far as to write a book on Brecht to prove that his political relationships with the contemporary world were foolish and unnecessary, and that behind all that he was really quite a sweet little bourgeois dreamer. Clearly, to these people theatre will have no relationship whatsoever with the question of 'news'. A story, a mediation of reality, is sold to the atomized alienated individuals of our society, as they retreat from engagement with that reality. The gentlemen at the head of the powerful opinion-forming corporations do not wish to have their articulate mediation of reality disturbed by a group of people going around with a different story, seeing events from a different perspective, even selecting different information. Still less do they wish to have the population at large emerging from their mental retreat – the inner exile of the powerless and alienated – and demanding a share of power, of control, of freedom. But these are precisely the areas that popular theatre can, and must, work in.

Any serious piece of theatre that questions all assumptions, that scrutinizes contemporary reality with a sense of history and without fear of engaging in politics, must inevitably tell a different story, with different values and a different perspective, from that received on the TV screen and from the pages of the *Sun*. Now the actual subject-matter of the show can be anything from two hundred years of the history of the working class of a particular region, to a chance encounter between a dislocated middle-class woman and a youth on a park-bench. The actual choice doesn't matter a great deal, as long as the situations are related outwards to discernible patterns, structures of society, historical realities that can connect with the audience's perception of reality and cause them to engage with it; as long as the perspective is thought through, not merely received, and the story is based on rigorous examination of experience, rather than the convenient fictions of the ruling class and its media.

Of course there are some kinds of general area of subject-matter that work better with a popular audience than others. The actual history of the working class, its formation, centuries of suffering and pride, the victories as the people moved towards a greater degree of emancipation, the distortions of purpose as they approached complete power, the lessons of the political struggles, the divisions within the people today and the mystification that prevails as the ruling class pretends it no longer rules. All this history has been suppressed, and needs to be shown to the people: it is a rich history, full of vivid episodes, songs, strong characters and plenty of action. Similarly, there are huge areas of contemporary life which are of major importance to the people of this country, but which are buried in mystery. The operation of the multinational corporations, the economics of technological progress, the politics of the micro-processor industry and its likely effects on leisure and employment prospects, the ongoing processes of sexual stereotyping, the uses and abuses of the spectre of Stalin, the use of the concept of 'freedom', as in free world and free enterprise – all these areas could form the basis for a piece of popular theatre, given the will and the skill and the imagination and the ingenuity required.

But I cannot prescribe the plots of possible plays. These I report as areas which I have found fruitful to work in or speculate on; others will no doubt have very different notions.

But one thing that this kind of theatre can be 'about' which is common to all good theatre is that extraordinary sense of the imaginative, creative leap out of alienated living that is communicated by a good performer in a good, but dangerous, part, as he or she takes the audience on a vertiginous adventure along the tightrope of invention and wit and imagination, the free man, or woman, free in the gaze of the audience, creating him or herself as they go along, surviving, and surpassing mere survival, taking the audience on into the concentrated world of the child at play, but bringing into play, as it were, the restless tokens of a changing reality. This role of theatre, this temporary, imaginative release from the chains of alienation and predictability, is perhaps one of the most important things that it is 'about', and can rarely be matched in intensity or presence by any other experience of art. It is this that can be ultimately the most subversive element in theatre, because it can create the appetite for throwing off those chains more frequently, for coming out of retreat and onto the offensive.

Clearly the starting point for any 'subject' has got to be the experience, skill and talent of the author or creators. We must never fall into the trap of trying to make mechanical theatre, with lumps of ideological Meccano. A person, or a very small group of people, has to be the human imaginative dimension through which the work is explored, mediated, created. Just as the set must relate

physically to the size of a person, and the auditorium
must be limited by the powers of projection of a person,
so the creation of theatre must pass through one coherent
mind in order to retain these dimensions, and to safe-
guard certain essential qualities that will allow it to enter
another human mind. We work within these limitations
because they define theatre, in basic, minimal terms.

So we start with an author – a playwright, a theatre-
maker. Here, perhaps, I can make a brief detour to take
in some problems of the writer's development that have
been raised. Now generally, given the class nature of education in this country, this indivudual will *begin* to write
or at least to conceive of writing, in the forms of high
culture. There have been some people who have begun by
writing pop songs, or wild west movies, or even TV
plays; but if we look a bit more closely at Dylan, or John
Lennon, the hallmark of literacy is there at the beginning, quite clearly. And I see no reason to oppose this in
the slightest. The least bourgeois education can give to
the working class is literary skill.

The imagination of anybody beginning to write will
usually run along the lines of some fashion or other from
the range of the dominant mode, and, depending on their
experience and originality of mind, the work will add to
that fashion, or transform it, or transcend it. And that's
all right too. But it is the job of anybody who wishes to
continue to write, particularly for the theatre, to extend
their experience, not only to observe but essentially to
live through as great a variety of experience as they can lay
claim to, to explore this experience in depth as well as in
breadth, and to find out, if possible at first hand, what is
going on in the world at large, and how their society
operates in particular. They must also find out, through
the work of others, how this society came about, and dis-
cover the history not only of the literature but also of the

people of their country, and the many strands and levels of behaviour that make up their culture, in the wider sense of that word.

Now the disciplines of writing essays, stories, short sketches and, in particular, poetry will help a writer develop confidence with ideas, and sensitivity to the powers and resources of language; the confident 'handling' of ideas, and 'sensitivity' to language are central, *sine qua non* – though not, in terms of theatre, ends in themselves. Language and intelligence must be set in motion in the larger terms of articulating one's growing experience of a particular society. It is that experience which must give a definition to one's work, that articulation which must give a tangible, specific feeling to one's writing, rather than some abstraction known as style.

It is important to acquire fresh skills, new methods of coping technically with new problems, and this can only be done by writing seriously, not by five-finger exercises, which never help a writer, excellent as they may be for a pianist. Working in other media, in television, radio, film, in poetry, song or polemic, can help to develop the writer's range of available resources. Looking at, participating in communal entertainment in all its many forms – in the dance-hall, the bingo-parlour, the wrestling stadium, the football match, the folk club, the parade, the circus, and so forth – will widen a writer's concept of the possible, will make the imagination richer and bolder. One's writing must cease to be holy, it must become a craft, a set of sturdy skills that are concrete and familiar, but never static, or complacent with themselves. Revision, rewriting under pressure, may be bad for the soul, but it brings an element of objectivity to one's job that strengthens the next assault on the inarticulate, gives one a basis for a small amount of self-confidence, a feeling of an apprenticeship being served the hard way, that few good writers have ever tried to avoid.

At this point I must direct this theory of creating theatre inwards, open it up towards the centre. For I do not believe that a great or even a good piece of theatre can emerge unless it has a level working coherently through it, or under it, which follows the path of a deeply felt, perhaps even an unconscious emotional struggle within the one person who is the creator of that piece of theatre. I refer back to my remarks about the need, in theatre, for the dimension of one person communicating through the work with one other person, the writer/creator communicating with each individual in the audience. I mentioned not only this dimension, but also certain specific qualities in a work, to allow it to pass from one mind to another in the right way. These qualities are to do with this emotional struggle-trajectory, this playing out of the deeply felt, the profoundly personal, through the other layers of theatre: through observed characters, social manners dissected, through conflict of classes and interests and so on. It is, to me, the element of magic, of primitive communication, that makes the whole business of theatre mean more than films, television, novels, even most poetry. It is the struggle-trajectory that binds the disparate elements of a work together, that tells you when to have a song, when to burst into violent action, when to draw the whole thing to a close. I suspect it to be very closely related to why some people write at all – agonizing as writing is – and others lead sane, healthy lives. Again, it is very much what a play is 'about' – even though neither the writer nor the audience may be fully conscious of exactly what it is.

It is at this point that I should reintroduce the two other elements in this set of forces, the audience, and the group of people with whom one is making theatre. Their introduction will not resolve anything, but will perhaps give us a more satisfactory set of determinations.

I believe – and I have spent some time in the first three of these lectures explaining why – that a writer (or director, actor or technician) coming into the theatre has to make a choice between working in bourgeois theatre with bourgeois values for largely middle-class audiences – and I include the trendy, experimental bits of the National and RSC as well as Bournemouth Rep. – and working in popular theatre with socialist values for largely working-class audiences. But 'working for' an audience is a very loose phrase. There are, as we noted earlier, various ways of relating to those audiences. In popular theatre the temptation is to trail along behind their tastes and interests in order to get an audience at all. I don't believe this is in fact necessary, and as we saw previously in talking about forms, there can be a process of development of form – and of content – during the course of a relationship between a company and an audience. I am not talking now particularly about 'leading' the audience towards complex ideas, etc. – this can and must be done from the very beginning. There is a way of handling an intellectually sophisticated notion as part of the structure of a show, without being patronizing or sounding like a schools programme. That way is to show the audience that they *need* this notion as members of a class whose future will be affected by it, or whose present has been shaped by it. In other words, if an idea, no matter how complex, can be seen to be a necessary weapon in a struggle, a popular audience will *want* to know about it. The imagination and skills of the writer, director and actors should be able to do the rest, provided they have built up a relationship of trust with the audience, and speak the language of the audience.

It may be objected that some ideas simply *cannot* be expressed in the language of such an audience, that the very form of such a theatre, working in short bursts, and a variety of styles, precludes many ideas. This may be true in the case of purely abstract ideas, but if an idea has any point of contact with reality at all, and if it means something in the context of their struggle to survive, a popular audience will grasp at least the essentials. For example, the rather complicated history of rationalization of industry with government support in the late 60s may not sound too promising for a joke-routine. But by the time, in 7:84 England's show, *Lay Off*, a large Irish actor had finished explaining, as Arnold Weinstock, just how beneficial to the country, or at least to GEC, this process was, and we had brought the news to the audience of how many people had been laid off, and where, to allow GEC to amalgamate, take over, rationalize and prosper, not only were the audience highly entertained by the manic and comic manoeuvres of Weinstock, but also they had grasped how this process affected their lives – in terms of jobs, and the products they can buy – and something of how structural unemployment is created by capitalist solutions to working-class problems. So when the show zoomed in on one individual who had been laid off, feeling upset in the launderette, and mucking about in the garden, that individual was seen as part of a major social process of change with technological, industrial and political determinations, rather than just as a poor unfortunate layabout as he might be presented in a senti- mental bourgeois drama. And the audience had grasped the essentials of the theoretical and historical ideas rele- vant to his – and possibly their – position.

But when I talk about tailism, or trailing along behind the audience, I mean in terms not only of the audience's understanding ideas, but also for the audience's ability to take criticism. Just as we need to reassess critically the forms of popular entertainment as we use them, so we must reassess our audience's ideology. The contradictions within the working class are many, and much of working-class life is backward and reactionary – not to say self-destructive – sexism, racism, authoritarianism, abuse of children, alcoholism, wilful intellectual self-mutilation, all these and worse are the working class's inheritance from the nineteenth century and their present condition. There is no point in becoming involved with the working class as the only social force capable of transforming society in a progressive manner, and simply *accepting* all these backward features and deformations. Therefore, I think, a great deal of popular theatre has got to be 'about' a socialist criticism of the audience. But is this possible without insulting or driving out the audience?

I believe it is, but it must be done from a position of basic political solidarity and cultural identity. The abuse heaped upon the working class by bourgeois ideologues over the years is no less offensive for being so totally hypocritical. Therefore an audience is simply not going to put up with ill-informed middle-class abuse. But of course there is a working-class perspective on its own position, and if the writer is aware of, draws strength from, and learns from the progressive elements in the working class, then a beginning can be made on some informed criticism which will be listened to.

In a show called *Out of Our Heads*, for example, the Scottish 7:84 toured working men's clubs and trades council clubs round central Scotland with a show about booze and the Scottish working man: how it went with the most sickening sexist attitudes, including physical abuse of wife and children, and became a pathetic substitute for some action which would try to remove the cancer of alienation that created the desire to drink in the first place. That was the social framework of the show, as it were. The formal framework was a development of the club forms, and as it was about the seventh show the company had done in Scotland, these forms had moved forward considerably from their original state towards a more subtle role in the creation of the show – but the audience still were familiar with what we were doing. And what was perhaps most important, the audience was familiar with *us*, as a company, and with what we stood for. And they approved of the standards of performance we had tried to maintain, in music, acting, lighting, etc. The audiences for that show were larger than for any previous show. I don't know what concrete differences it made to men's drinking habits – maybe some, temporary ones – but it certainly made a difference to people's attitudes to the situation of battered women in Scotland, and to the refuges. But on a deeper level, the presence of this kind of theatre, critically reflecting the lives and aspirations of the people of a country, can, if successful and dynamic, create a climate of moving forward, of self-confidence, of debate on many levels, can begin to move the main thrust of working-class activity beyond trades union economism, and start to raise other questions without which the achievement of socialism becomes meaningless, particularly in the developed countries.

I believe theatre can best achieve its independent artistic objectives by becoming a part of this hugely complex movement towards a developed, sophisticated but liberating form of socialism which is happening all over Europe, East and West, and in many other parts of the world. Without it, the end of the twentieth century is going to be a grim time to be alive. This does not mean that I insist that all plays should be recruiting meetings for a party that doesn't exist. It is simply that to be good as *theatre*, plays now must ruthlessly question their ideological bases, the set of assumptions about life on which they are built, and should have a questioning, critical relationship with their audience, based on trust, cultural identification and political solidarity. These attitudes behind the work are always what plays are really 'about'. The subject-matter, as I've said, can then relate to the areas of life likely to produce the richest response from the writer's creative imagination, and to mean the most to one's specific audience.

The spectacle of the bourgeois artist desperately trying to curry favour with posterity by turning away from the present is a comic spectacle, and not one to produce either good theatre, or a better society.

6

The Challenge of
Cinema and Television

I suppose what I have been trying to do is to analyse the contemporary theatre scene in the light of my own experience and political perspective, and to give an account of one possible way through to a different kind of theatre. We saw that while some of the content of some of the plays written in the dominant theatre tradition may appear to 'contest' the bourgeois state, their context, the language of their presentation, their form, the event which they are part of, all serve to legitimize the bourgeois state, all have, as it were, their hands in the till. I postulated as an alternative to this dominant, vigorous and rich mode, an emergent mode of theatre – it has indeed been emergent for many years – which speaks the language of working-class entertainment and tries to develop that language to make critical, progressive theatre primarily for popular audiences. I tried to describe some of the characteristics of this kind of theatre, and in the last lecture talked about *some* of the values such a theatre might contain.

Today I should like to try – briefly – to look at the way this form could develop, under the pressure of the subject-matter which it will be called upon to contain. I should like also to try to put the relationship between formal development and subject matter in the context of the other dramatic media – film and television – and their possibilities.

I think perhaps the best place to start this task is to look at a conventional, but sympathetic, attitude to theatre from a socialist writer. Writing in a preface to two of his television plays, Trevor Griffiths says:

> Of all the outlets available to a playwright for his work, television seems to me at once the most potent and the most difficult; the most potent and *therefore* the most difficult, one's inclined to add. Film boasts a 'global audience' (as one celebrated English director put it, perhaps as a way of justifying his new Californian existence) but has never afforded the writer a status in the power-structure much above that of, say, a second-unit director. With relatively few exceptions, film uses (and has usually always attracted) writers for whom wealth and ease and a certain sort of localized (i.e. American) celebrity are or have become inseparable from the writing impulse itself; so that the consequential loss of regard (and self-regard) will be measured against more tangible and presumably more consumable gains. The global audience will then be surrendered by the writer to the expert ministrations of other 'ideas men': studio chiefs ('We could have bought into North Sea oil with what we paid for this shit'), distributors ('It's too long/short/frank'), directors ('Do I get the cut?'), stars ('I *know* what they want. They want me.') and so on.
>
> Theatre is in important ways the converse; that's to say, while at its most secure it offers the writer a greater degree of control than any other medium over the production of his work, it is incapable, as a social institution, of reaching, let alone *mobilizing*, large popular audiences, at least in what is more and more desperately referred to as the Free World. Success in the theatre can confer fame, prestige, wealth, critical acciaim and a place in literature, but all of them will be pickled in a sort of class aspic. To write only for the theatre is to watch only from the covered stand; you

stay dry but there's a pitch dividing you from another possible, and possibly decisive, action on the terraces.

There are fewer cinemagoers in Britain now than there are anglers; fewer regular theatregoers than car-rallyers. For most people, plays are television plays, 'drama' is television drama (though it's a word used almost exclusively by those responsible for *production*, rarely if ever by audiences). A play on television, transmitted by mid-evening on a weekday, will make some sort of contact with anything from three to twelve million people (twenty if it's a series), usually all at the same time.

I have quoted from Trevor Griffiths at length because I'm sure he is voicing a thought which does occur to many serious writers and critics and students, and to many actors, directors and technicians when they go to or work in the theatre.

My reply to this position is really to agree with it in so far as one accepts theatre as a static, unchangeable entity, an entrée to Literature, a cosmopolitan bourgeois culture-product. Incidentally, this notion of art reached one of its great apogees in Paris recently, when the new, three-act version of Berg's *Lulu* was opened at the Paris Opéra in the presence of the world's opera-merchants, and the Prime Minister of France, Chancellor Schmidt of West Germany and our own Edward Heath, assembled to complete the acquisition of Alban Berg, the reviled composer, Frank Wedekind, the dangerous playwright, and Lulu, the whore, by the international cultural community. This in the same week that President Carter had an émigré Russian ballet dancer perform in the White House, and declare that such art transcends human differences. However, to return to Trevor Griffiths's position.

First of all, as we have seen, the theatre is neither static, nor unchangeable. It is possible to make a theatre of the terraces – indeed, many of us have been doing so for some years. It is wrong to define theatre in terms of the RSC and the National, just as it is wrong to define cinema in terms of big-budget Hollywood movies. The problem, however, with alternative kinds of theatre, and cinema, is that they involve a diminution of scale – of cash, of resources, (therefore of talent), and certainly of recognition in the bourgeois press. In the case of the cinema, this shortage of cash can make life impossible – any film costs a lot of money, and if it is to be distributed commercially to recoup its costs, it requires to satisfy certain requirements of the commercial cinema chains, or of the major distributors. These requirements frequently – one is tempted to say invariably – negate the whole meaning of the film. We shall come back to this situation later. In the meantime, let us note that in terms of availability of cash and resources, the theatre *at the moment* is easier to work in.

If a writer, director or actor wishes to work in alternative theatre, and has something to offer, there are companies crying out for him or her. I'm sure most of you will know by now the story of the rise of the touring theatre companies between 1968 and 1975, and the creation of smaller, alternative theatres in many towns, and the growth of theatre in education, and community theatre. The fact that the Arts Council financed this blooming of a hundred flowers, or whatever it was, indicated very clearly that within a liberal or social-democratic structure, the contradictions of society will find expression, will produce contradictions within that structure, as indeed they should. A new, hard-working and enterprising kind of theatre emerged, not from nowhere, but from a fusion of many past traditions and experiences – like those of Joan Littlewood, the Unity theatres, the Workers Theatre Movement of the 30s, the political theatre of Brecht, Piscator, O'Casey, Odets and many others – a fusion of these traditions and experiences firstly with a new, de-Stalinised, liberationist, activist way of working on the Left, and above all with an upsurge of militancy within the working class in Britain starting with the fight against 'In Place of Strife' and culminating in the victory at Saltley Gates. A theatre emerging from such a fusion *had* to be a theatre of the terraces, *had* to and *did* play to, and help to mobilize, large popular audiences, did contribute a depth of cultural meaning to the working-class movement, and indeed continues to do so, but under changed conditions. To the pressure of that upsurge of work, the Arts Council responded with small amounts of money, which, as the Arts Council recognized the value of the work, increased a little bit – but never to a high enough level to allow this kind of theatre to challenge the dominant mode in size. It was kept as a kind of vast recruiting-ground for the RSC and the National and the bigger reps – a junior subsidiary of the monolith. Even so, such an alternative theatre found the cash, resources, the degree of freedom and the audiences necessary to make a significant intervention.

Cinema, on the other hand, has rarely found the necessary cash or resources to be available without a crushing of the necessary freedom. As Maurice Hatton's film *Long Shot* indicates, most British 'independent' film makers put all their effort into finding compromising solutions to non-problems. This does not mean that the effort to make oppositional films is not worthwhile – just a lot harder. There are organizations like the BFI Production Board and indeed the Arts Council, with limited funds available to help finance independent films, but sadly the general level of confidence, experience and skill tends to be so low that very little of value emerges.

There is a further problem with cinema in this country,

which is that it has been defined by Hollywood and its satellites in this country. There is undoubtedly a mass working-class audience for cinema. But it has expectations of what it will get, indeed specific formal demands, which, if unsatisfied, will leave the audience in confusion, at the very least. Now there is a school of thought, present in many of the assumptions behind *Screen* magazine, and expressed in it by Geoffrey Nowell-Smith as follows: 'To my mind the role of American cultural forms in British cultural life has in the past been broadly progressive, if only because of the overtly reactionary character of much British so-called popular culture'. Admittedly he sees the possibility that the American 'invasion' may simply have reinforced British forms of reaction, but even this is not nearly enough to characterize the defining effect that Hollywood has had on the expectations of a British popular audience from the cinema as a cultural experience, and as a way of mediating reality. In fact, the whole idea that Hollywood's role has been 'broadly progressive' is absolute rubbish; Hollywood has simply made the task of 'popularizing' progressive cinema a million times more difficult than that of creating progressive popular theatre. On the whole the theatre has excluded popular audiences so rigorously, that the idea of popular theatre is graspable and politically meaningful in the way that the idea of 'popular cinema' is not.

Of course, popular cinema has existed in other societies, and revolutionary popular cinema has created great works, in the past, and no doubt it will again in the future: everything changes.

There is another way of looking at the cinema as a place to work in, which for a time I subscribed to: that one could work within the confines of commercial cinema to send out signals to audiences, to record areas of life and experience in which the urge to communicate overlapped the demands of the movie moguls. I spent eight months of my life working on a screenplay of Malraux's *La Condition Humaine* – an account of the workers' uprising in Shanghai in 1927, and their massacre at the hands of their allies, the Kuo-Min Tang. It is a great novel in many ways, and to work on such a period of history with that novel as a medium seemed very exciting and worth doing at that time, not least as a counter-balance to the anti-Mao and pro-Chiang-Kai-Chek propaganda in the Free World: this was in 1967, the year of the Cultural Revolution. Of course it was never made. Malraux, by then Minister of Culture in De Gaulle's cabinet, hooked on opium, and afraid of the use to which the film might be put, disavowed his youth, asked for the semi-autobiographical central character to be removed, and complained that the script emphasized the political and was not 'philosophical' enough. Now this is clearly a high level piece of censorship, with a conscious political content, and, as such, one really doesn't mind it so much. But in other films which I have written and which have been made, a much more insidious form of distortion takes place. I was interested to watch, ten years later, the performance of Rachel Roberts in *The Reckoning*. Although the script called for a woman who knew her own mind but was trapped in savage economic circumstances, Rachel Roberts gave a picture of that woman which was completely male-oriented, subservient and mindless. Why? Not because the director had demanded such a distortion – though clearly he went along with it – but because of her whole 'training' in the cinema. Indeed, I first saw her giving a picture of Polly Garter in *Under Milk Wood* that was every bit as sentimental, sexist and cynical as Dylan Thomas's own writing of the character. But in that performance, and in *The Reckoning*, there remained remarkable traces of her own real experience that made the distortions of the rest all the more agonizing.

Now I quote Rachel Roberts' performance because of this contradiction. There is no doubt that she *could* have played a real, unsentimentalized woman; but years of fighting up the ladder the hard way had conditioned her to use her undoubted intelligence to work out a way to play the part that allowed her a certain amount of dignity, but which went a long way to conform to a 'Polly Garter' image of woman that commercial cinema had taught her was her specific saleable commodity, and which was what she had been hired for that film to deliver.

This type of calculation is unconscious in many performers, though it is very conscious in the very successful. But it indicates that in every little nook and cranny of the practice of cinema within the orbit of Hollywood, there lurks an ideology. To imagine, as I once did, that one can 'use' this kind of cinema to do something that is opposed to that ideology, is to ignore the fact that every single stage of the process, from Wall Street financier to distributor to producer to stars to director to camera-crew to editor's floor-sweeper is saturated in that ideology. Every single stage in the process will shift the meaning irreversibly towards the reactionary consensus, which has already been sold over and over again to the audience as 'cinema' – a night at the pictures. To challenge this, every single stage in the process becomes the site of a savage ideological struggle, and *then*, if you succeed, the audience will not be getting what it wants.

Of course this argument is hopelessly undialectical. The struggle within cinema is real, there *are* forces in society that can and do respond to a different kind of cinema, these forces can expand, can generalize this taste, or need, through several layers of society – and the effort to achieve a revolutionary cinema may in the end succeed

– but there will, of course, need to be certain hard-fought-for changes within the institutions of cinema, and in the distribution of social forces within our society, for this to happen.

In this country, then, at this moment, I think there are greater possibilities for a new kind of creative work in the theatre than in the cinema, either outside or inside the commercial sphere. On the other hand, the cinema is an important popular medium, and it could well be argued that as it *does* reach many millions more people than theatre, then one has a certain responsibility towards it, and one ought to fight in all ways possible to claim it as a medium of the people, rather than a medium that celebrates capitalist values while exploiting the people. In order to do this, in my opinion, cinema will first have to reorganize itself financially and industrially so that a film made in Britain stands a fair chance of recouping 80–90 per cent of its costs from British audiences. At the moment this is virtually impossible, the only exception being very cheap and very nasty 'sexploitation' or *Confessions of a Window Cleaner*-type films. Almost all other commercial films (i.e. films with budgets over £100,000) are aimed, whether we like it or not, at some so-called 'international' market, which in reality is the huge cinema-going masses of the USA. Excellent as they may be, they have very little active interest in the present problems, specific history or cultural developments of the British working class, or indeed of any European people: why should they? Cinema, of course, is supposed to rise to the level of myth, of timeless, classless narrative with a meaning which has no reference outside itself, hidden from all but the high priests of semiology. But even accepting that certain narratives can transcend a local or national context, the context must be *there*, it is the language-system of the narrative, it is also the point of reference outwards to an interested judging audience, and the point of reference inward, the route along which events, characters and meanings travel into the actual, realized film. The context of a social art-form like cinema, or theatre, must be a defined society, or community. Now to try to create a film about, say, Moss Side in Manchester, while constantly translating the story into an artefact which will pander to the entertainment values and general interests of a mentally retarded mid-Western sex criminal – which, on occasion, I have been called upon to do – is an exercise which benefits neither the writer, the local community, nor the great US film-going public. On the other hand, to make films rooted in their context, referring to the British working class as subject, as well as audience, is to be doomed to inadequate funds. Kevin Brownlow attempted, with BFI backing, to make a film, based on David Caute's *Comrade Jacob*, about Winstanley, an English primitive Communist, and the Diggers, who took the English Civil War in 1649 way beyond the demands of the bourgeoisie and Cromwell into demanding that all land and property be held in common and organized locally for the benefit of all – an extraordinarily vivid, and instructive period of English history. The film that emerged, desperately underfinanced, poorly acted, badly shot and put together, is doomed to the cineastical ghetto whose mentality encases it. It has had no impact whatsoever on the working-class movement: the publication by Penguin of a collection of Winstanley's writings is a much more effective contribution to the political situation, and even that is fairly minimal.

It would be nice to think of a British cinema which was answerable to its own audience, which explored the lives, the experiences, the rich imaginations, the mythologies, the history of the British people, which can grow from those roots to whatever heights its makers can take their audiences up to. It may appear like arrant chauvinism, but I don't think British films will ever be any good, or even exist at all, unless and until they can be made with both eyes fixed on a British audience. This may mean reducing costs, which will be resisted by the unions, or increasing government subsidy, which will be resisted by the Treasury, the Tories and many Labour ministers, or a string of huge domestic successes, which doesn't look like happening without either or both of the previous conditions being met.

One solution to both financing and distributing British two-dimensional drama is, of course, British television. Once again, we must remember that everything changes, that liberal regimes come and go, that the present situation won't, thank God, last forever.

However, it might well have occurred to some of you, as it occurred to Trevor Griffiths, and as it did indeed occur to me some time ago, that television is, or should be, the popular medium *par excellence*.

Now I have a great deal to say about television, but I must try to restrict my comments to the relationship it bears to contemporary theatre, or we shall be here all week. Television drama is a greatly under-explored area. Most of the attempts to grapple with it seem to me to have either misunderstood or ignored completely the nature of the production processes, and most seem to misunderstand the nature of the communication taking place: but television drama, in this country at least, exists as a relatively powerful social force and as a challenge to every dramatic writer who is at all concerned with writing for a mass audience. We all know how important, how central to the legitimation of the industrial, centralized state command structure an efficient, state-controlled television service has become. As Enzensberger has remarked, in a *coup d'état* or in a revolution, those in search of power occupy the broadcasting studios first, the presidential palace second. The retention of power by de Gaulle over the French television and radio networks in 1968 gave him his victory, not the generals in Germany. The extraordinary contradiction of a commercial station, Europe 1, broadcasting live coverage of the street fighting in Paris in 1968, however, built up the numbers taking part better than any number of politically correct pamphlets. After about 1971, the British government, acting on experience of de-escalation in Belfast, suddenly simply did not show film of demonstrations, rallies, acts of civil disobedience, etc. in this country. Equally suddenly, demos went out of fashion. They still are. The government's previous tactic had been to show demonstrators as 'freaks', selecting the most outrageously idiotic costume on the fringe of an otherwise sober march to represent the silliness of such protests. They miscalculated badly, because this actually attracted a lot of people to the demo. Silence, the bleak face of Richard Baker grimly denouncing by the relationship between his teeth, upper lip and the tip of his nose, the absent, unimagineably grey and boring fanatics who disrupt the traffic, combined with their absence from the screen, has achieved what the Metropolitan Police alone could never have managed: apathy. Non-events.

Therefore I propose to examine, briefly, drama on television on the basis of what is absent from it, as this absence is more significant than a thousand liberal gestures.

First of all, a play, or series, which relates a human tragedy or misery or alienation or madness or deprivation, to a *social structure* is almost completely absent from our screens. Second, any attempt to present society (or even any group of people) as having any control over its future, as having any genuine choice between different ways of creating its future, is extremely rare. Third, in terms of the class struggle, any historical drama in which the working class actually wins a victory is a rarity, almost an impossibility. Try suggesting a play about Saltley Gates to Alisdair Milne. Fourth, a play in which the actors express themselves as human beings, with opinions about life, not just as sweet faces or quaint voices ingratiating themselves with the public and the directors by doing what they are told with as much charm as they can muster – such plays and occasions are unheard of. Finally, any dramatic convention which encourages, points to, or even allows any historical, social, theoretical or technological level of thinking to take place during the course of a drama, is clearly not suitable for television, and will not be seen on your screen.

Furthermore, it is very important to grasp the nature of the communication which television as an object will allow. It is essentially a piece of furniture. Even with 625 lines, looking at a film on it, compared with seeing it in the cinema, is like listening to a performance of a symphony over the telephone. It just doesn't compare with the real thing. Also, television programmes very rarely begin and end; they emerge from a burble of other things on the tube, and in one's life, and slide back into burble. Rarely do they cause a deep rethinking of one's whole philosophy of life, or even encourage one to give any simple programme a second thought, it's: 'And now, *The Old Grey Whistle Test*' or 'Turn that thing off and put the kettle on, dear' – rather than a ruminative silence in which Western literature is reordered in the light of this new addition to it. In other words, television-watching is a frame of mind, and the technically sub-standard pictures, the reality of the medium as a piece of furniture, and the inconsequentiality built into it as an experience, all conspire to set severe limits on that frame of mind, on what effort we are prepared to put into, and what depth of rewarding experience we are expecting to take out of, the time spent watching TV. Indeed, for many people it is no more than a way of passing time painlessly, or a way of keeping the mind soothed while the body recovers from a day's work. It goes with carpet slippers, cocoa and biscuits to nibble; it is an amenity, like soft toilet-paper.

Even so, television has power. In the politically sensitive areas like News and Current Affairs, straightforward and articulate political control over programme-makers is exercised. I find working in these areas, which I do quite frequently, quite refreshing, because at least you can argue about the real issues, and the producer will expect you to, and respect you for it. In drama, however, nothing is straightforward, you're not supposed to argue, and political control is exercised by a dim-witted, inarticulate appeal to 'commonsense', or the consensus, or a shared fear of Mrs Whitehouse. But still, TV drama has power, especially the series, in forming public opinion on a fairly trivial level, and in reinforcing stereotypes, but above all, in defining 'normality' – that most powerful of concepts in a frightened society.

Now to make television drama which challenges accepted ideas of the 'normal', that raises specific social problems, or reveals layers of working-class history, or that even contains an oppositional ideology is, very occasionally, quite possible in BBC-TV, and on Thames and Granada TV with a greater effort. We should be very aware that this is not possible on any other television network that I know of in the free world outside Scandinavia and a few hours on one subscription channel in Holland. Therefore it is important to ensure that the freedom enjoyed in this area is safeguarded, and used to its best advantage. The serious writer in television at the moment must:

1. analyse the real nature of television communication, and the processes of material and ideological production;

2. intervene in the situation in order to challenge the stifling 'TV naturalist' form that reduces the world either to a small bowl of emotional stew, handed out in weekly dollops, or to a series of criminal acts performed by deviants who end up shot by our hero, or lead off weeping to the loony-bin;

3. re-assert the possibility of forms in television which do allow a small degree of theoretical thinking into the act of creation and communication, which allow for a world picture that involves the working of the human mind rather than the automatic operation of convenient prejudice;

4. create vigorously and well, with an awareness of the limitations of the medium, in such a way as to command a deeper response from a popular audience;

5. use words, images, ideas with a historical awareness as well as an awareness of the audience;

6. create a world where events have reasons, where the past determinations of the present are shown in all their complexity, and the present's determination of the future is seen as a series of human choices;

7. enrich the audience's awareness of the possibilities of humanity, through play and the imagination as well as through work, through communication and community as well as through solitary achievement.

But let me quote, against that, an extract from Enzensberger:

Real democracy, as opposed to the formal facades of parliamentary democracy, does not exist anywhere in the world, but its ghost haunts every existing regime. Consequently, all the existing power structures must seek to obtain the consent, however passive, of their subjects. Even regimes which depend on the force of arms for their survival feel the need to justify themselves in the eyes of the world. Control of capital, of the means of production, and of the armed forces is therefore no longer enough. The self-appointed élites who run modern societies must try to control people's minds. What each of us accepts or rejects, what we think and decide is now, here as well as in Vietnam, a matter of prime political concern: it would be too dangerous to leave these matters to ourselves. Material exploitation must camouflage itself in order to survive; immaterial exploitation has become its necessary corollary. The few cannot go on accumulating wealth unless they accumulate the power to manipulate the minds of the many. To expropriate manpower they have to expropriate the brain. What is being abolished in today's affluent societies, from Moscow to Los Angeles, is not exploitation, but our awareness of it. . . .

In order to exploit people's intellectual, moral and political faculties, you have got to develop them first. This is, as we have seen, the basic dilemma faced by today's media. When we turn our attention from the industry's consumers to its producers, the intellectuals, we find this dilemma aggravated and intensified. In terms of power, of course, there can be no question as to who runs the business. Certainly it is not the intellectuals who control the industrial establishment, but the establishment which controls them. There is precious little chance for the people who are productive to take over their means of production: this is just what the present structure is designed to prevent. However, even under present circumstances, the relationship is not without a certain ambiguity, since there is no way of running the mind industry without enlisting the services of at least a minority of people who can create something. . . . This is an industry which has to rely, as its primary source, on the very minorities with whose elimination it is entrusted: those whose aim it is to invent and produce *alternatives*. Unless it succeeds in exploiting and manipulating its producers, the mind industry cannot hope to exploit and manipulate its consumers. On the level of production, even more than on the level of consumption, it has to deal with partners who are potential enemies. Engaged in the proliferation of human consciousness, the media proliferate their own contradictions.

So television, as I said, presents massive challenges to those who make it, particularly the writers. Although these challenges overlap in several important areas with those made to the theatre-maker, I think it is vital to see these areas of writing activity as very different, but not mutually exclusive. It is a matter of debate within every writer as to which area is right to work in at any given point, having regard to the state of both media, the situation in the country, and the state of the writer's creative juices. I would hesitate to recommend television as a full-time occupation for a writer, though. It is, as they say, a voracious maw, a machine that needs endlessly feeding. It induces in its servants a jackdaw mentality – if it glistens, pick it up, pop it in the nest – which may be OK for those poor rich people who snaffle up jokes for the TV comedians all day and every day, but is hardly conducive to a rewarding life-time's work.

The theatre, particularly if it is as close to its audience as I think it should be, will feed you back more than it takes. An ongoing, trusting relationship with an audience, any live audience I suppose, but particularly a popular audience, will give strength and courage, and new ways of seeing things, and a fresh imagination, and endless facts and information, and a constantly developing, tested-out theoretical level, and a whole lot of human kindness, generosity and solidarity, to writer and theatre company alike. If a writer in theatre does not love his or her audience, he or she will die. It can be a critical love, an aggressive love, but if it turns to indifference, cynicism, hate, or simply exploitation, then the theatre-maker will turn into a solipsist or a psychopath: for mankind to have a better future, neither is very helpful.

I'd like to end by saying to those of you who intend to try to work in theatre, or film, or television, that simply by being here in Cambridge you are already on the conveyor-belt to a position in the dominant culture, a well-rewarded place in the service of the ruling class. It may well be what you want, that's your decision: the point is, that you will in fact be faced with a series of decisions, which will not present themselves as decisions; they will occur as natural moves in the process of entering the world, matters of 'common sense'. All I would ask is that those of you who do enter the theatre see every step as the site of serious struggle, which calls for well-informed and principled decisions. Then at least you will have created your own future.

Appendix

1971–2

The company began its life with a production of John McGrath's *Trees In The Wind* at the Edinburgh Festival in August 1971, which then toured around England, Wales and Scotland with the help of a small grant from the Arts Council and a lot of unpaid work from many of the people who presented us, and a large but hidden subsidy from those who worked for the company on less than subsistence wages.

During the next year, we mounted and toured five major productions of plays by Trevor Griffiths, John Arden and Margaretta D'Arcy, and myself. In addition there was a lunchtime show and several appearances at rallies, including shows for the Edinburgh Trades Council's May Day rally, and in an occupied factory in Glasgow.

What started out as an attempt to make socialist theatre became during this time an attempt to make theatre of and for the working class in a socialist way. (Most of the major formal innovations or rediscoveries that I discuss in the third, fourth and fifth chapters of this book took place, for me at least, in three main periods – the first at Liverpool Everyman in 1970–1; the second with both 7:84 companies during 1972–6; and the third with 7:84 Scotland during 1979/80.)

This first year and a half of 7:84's work was organized from the front room of my house, with everyone working for the company getting the same wage – never more than £28 per week – and me receiving no wage at all. We carried sets, costumes and lights for two productions at a time in one second-hand 18 cwt. Ford Transit van, with a roof-rack and a charmed existence. Actors travelled in borrowed cars, until, in September 72, we bought a mini-bus in Stirling.

Most venues were one-nighters – and the travelling was monumental: overnight from Lancaster to Swansea, Liverpool to Devon, all in the era of minimal motorways.

From enthusiastic autocracy at the beginning (Trevor Griffiths once referred to me as 'il Duce') to a *form* of collective control, within a year, was not bad going: meetings, endless meetings became part of our weekly schedule, held in basements in Rotherham, board-rooms in Aberdeen, once in the back of a truck – and in countless smoke-heavy dressing-rooms the length of the island. We discussed just about everything, from the growth of the nation-state to nylon sheets, by way of 'what we ought to be doing is . . .', and 'what are we in this dump for?'

Among the people – my apologies to those omitted – who worked with us in those first eighteen months, were: Victor Henry, Elizabeth MacLennan (now of 7:84 Scotland), Gillian Hanna (now of Monstrous Regiment), Feri Lean and David MacLennan (now of Wildcat) and Sandy Craig (of *Time Out*, editor of book on alternative theatre), Gavin Richards (now of Belt and Braces,) Tony Haygarth (as seen on TV), Stephen Rea, Roger Sloman, Vari Sylvester, Shane Connaughton, Deborah Norton, Tamara

Hinchco, Peter Sproule, John Joyce, Paul Kessel and many others who continue to make their very individual and remarkable contributions to the theatre. The shows were directed by Alan Dosser, Richard Eyre, Gavin Richards and myself, and the sets and props made by Nick Redgrave, who still makes them today.

The critics were on the whole very enthusiastic about our work in those days, but even then complaints about 'preaching' and 'dogmatism' were made by those who chose not to have their prejudices examined, their pre-judgements questioned. But we were given considerable coverage and a great deal of praise, all of which helped Sue Timothy in the Arts Council to justify giving us money, and made 7:84 a good place for young actors to be seen doing exciting new plays with up-and-coming direc-tors, all over the country – in spite of the wages.

And the audiences came in, in the universities where the students were mad for left-wing theatre, in the disused school in Rochdale, the gym in Preston, where the people were starved of any theatre at all.

1972–3

Then, between December 72, and March 73, things changed very rapidly. *The Ballygombeen Bequest*, the Arden/D'Arcy play, was taken off three days before the end of a sixteen-week tour because of a threatened libel action. Both it and its companion piece, my adaptation of Arden's *Musgrave*, had touched on the situation in Nor-thern Ireland; although both sharply attacked the Provis-ional IRA, both also attacked British policy.

As a result of the legal tangle we lost three days' income: though Arden and D'Arcy subsequently lost a lot more, before the wretched case was settled out of court.

As a result of attacking the British military's activities

in certain prisons in Ireland (accusations we made have since been upheld in the European Court), nevertheless we lost our chance of a sizeable annual grant from the Arts Council. We were forced to stagger on from show to show with no cash in between the end of one tour and the start of rehearsal for the next, and no guarantee that any more would come anyway.

So in December the *Ballygombeen/Musgrave* tour ended in disarray, the company dispersed with no definite plans for the future, and most of them went off quite rightly to work elsewhere.

During the first two months of 73 discussion raged, and ended with a meeting at which it was decided that Gavin Richards should seize an opportunity that arose and start what became Belt and Braces, that the English lot should stay in London to do a tour of Adrian Mitchell's *Man Friday*, and that David MacLennan, Feri Lean, Elizabeth MacLennan and I should go to Scotland to start a Scottish company. These things we all did.

1973–5

What happened with Belt and Braces is not my story to tell. The English 7:84 put on a very good tour of *Man Friday* in a mixture of working-class venues and small community gigs, and theatres, including the Cambridge Arts Theatre. But after this tour, and a troubled co-production with Belt and Braces, the English company went into a curious decline for nearly a year.

Meanwhile the Scottish 7:84 began its life with a company of performers and a show and a sense of excitement that swept through almost the whole of the country, and since, on TV, through the whole of Britain, Ireland, Norway, Sweden, even New Zealand and Australia. With *The Cheviot, the Stag and the Black, Black Oil*, I felt I was just beginning to work in the way I had hoped to be able to work when the whole thing began. The show was about the Highlands, from the clearances to the oil boom, and in a set of sketches, songs and direct statements, it related the experiences of the Highlanders to the demands of capital, and showed vividly the central contradiction between what the people wanted – and want – and what capital inflicts on them. The form (of the *ceilidh*) was an adaptation of the traditional form of entertainment of the Highlands, the music was what the people liked, and the songs, in Gaelic and English, went to the root of suppressed popular feeling.

This show played for many months round small towns and villages in the north of Scotland, the Hebrides, the Orkneys, then into Glasgow Citizens Theatre, and eventually the Abbey Dublin, and a tour of the West of Ireland – Shannon, Galway, Westport and Sligo. There was instant affinity between the Irish audiences and what we were saying and the way we were saying it. Demands for an Irish company to do similar work were made loudly, and the Scottish company still goes back to Ireland and always that rapport is immediately revived.

We also represented Scotland in Brussels, in the Europalia, to the evident distaste of the British Council's man there, and the delight of large audiences, amongst whom was Ritsaert ten Cate of the Mickery Theatre, Amsterdam, who has invited us to Amsterdam many times since.

But we went back from Brussels to Scourie, a village on the north coast of Scotland, and continued our main work. This was not to be only with remote communities in the Outer Hebrides – though they are very important, and not to be under-estimated, or written off by David Edgar as 'peasants'.

Our next show in Scotland was *The Game's a Bogey*, about which I talk in the fourth lecture. With it we built the industrial working-class audience in Scotland that is our main support and from which we draw what strength we have.

I shan't go on to catalogue the rest of our work in Scotland during these years. We went back to the Highlands several times, but mostly we toured the miners' clubs, community centres, school halls, theatres and trades council clubs of central Scotland and the eastern industrial areas of Dundee and Aberdeen. The work we have done in them is central to this book.

Back in England, however, things were not happening, until a small group who believed the work of the company to be very important resurrected the English 7:84 to fame and fortune with a production of a play I wrote for the Everyman called *Fish in The Sea*, which Pam Brighton directed magnificently and for which Mark Brown wrote new music which was very exciting.

This opened in London's Half Moon, and received great critical acclaim. It toured to, and was taken into, the heart of Liverpool's Scotland Road, and we began to find in England a similar reaction to the one we were getting in Scotland. The new group of actors and musicians, who had now joined the older ones, contained some who were equally dedicated to the company and the audiences: Colm Meany was one, and Mike O'Neill, piano-player and composer was another.

1975–6
In March 75 the English 7:84 was finally given an annual grant by the Arts Council, and we immediately formed a company of six actors and four musicians and started the most exciting year's work in the English company's history. *Lay Off* was a polemic with theatrical pyrotechnics on the subject of the multinationals; *Yobbo Nowt* was a 'musical comedy' about a woman who finds her way from subjection in a stifling marriage to political and per-

sonal consciousness. Both shows did over a hundred performances, and went everywhere – to occupied factories, town halls, Communist Party rallies, Socialist Worker Party branches, Unity Theatre, the Shaw Theatre, Glasgow Citizens, Amsterdam, Manchester, South Wales. *Rat Trap*, a shorter show about inflation, even played the Royal Festival Hall, packed for a rally.

The Scottish Company went on with *Little Red Hen* and *Honour Your Partners* (7:84's contribution to the bicentennial celebrations), drawing ever bigger audiences, and also getting an annual grant from the Scottish Arts Council.

During these years we managed to move the offices out of people's front rooms and, in Edinburgh, into a small room with a view over the Forth in Queen Street, and in London first into the basement of a flower shop, then into a windowless cell in a converted warehouse in Clerkenwell. We also acquired slightly bigger trucks to carry the sets, and slightly more reliable transport for the company. We pushed the wages up a bit as well – living below subsistence level is fine for a year or two, but becomes self-defeating after a time, and it gets more difficult to persuade people to do it as the years go by.

The fact is, both companies are doing the job that the Arts Council was set up for, and both should have enough money to do that job efficiently and to pay reasonable wages to those with the skills to work in this area. There is a general feeling, not only amongst right-wing Tories, that this kind of work is 'fringe' and should remain in a financial ghetto, in case it grows big enough to challenge the established values of theatre – that it should content itself with being a low-paid training area for talent to be picked off and misused by the 'real' theatre. Fortunately the Scottish Arts Council does not hold this view, but there is growing evidence that the Drama Department of the English Arts Council thinks along these or similar lines. We feel very strongly that the taxes which finance the Arts Council come from all sections of the community and that the working class and those of all classes who happen *not* to live in a large town get very little back from the Arts Council for their money, apart from us and other touring theatre.

1977–8

These were problematic years for both companies. While the audiences continued to want the shows, internal wrangling in England, and in Scotland the break-up, mainly through sheer exhaustion, of the nucleus of people who created the company's identity in the early years, led to great difficulties and strains. In addition, in England the shows went into a decline for a time, and the performing standards were not good. The answer we found in Scotland was to have a year off to think (during two months of which I went to Cambridge to deliver the lectures in this book).

In England the solution was not so direct or so sensible. We struggled on, after splits and disagreements, and continued to provide entertainment with a familiar form and a socialist perspective to popular audiences. In 1978 we revived an earlier play of mine, *Underneath*, which Pam Brighton directed for us, and then Margaretta D'Arcy and John Arden produced a play we commissioned from them called *Vandaleur's Folly*, an Anglo-Irish melodrama involving the Ralahine co-operative, the early days of the Orange Order, the evils of gambling and a great deal else besides. The English company still continues to present new socialist plays with a relevance to the lives of the people in the audience.

1979–80

In 1979, after a year's break, the Scottish 7:84 went back into action with *Joe's Drum*, and the audiences responded to it vigorously – not always in agreement, but, generally speaking, involved. And the Scottish 7:84 continued, with *Swings and Roundabouts*, to pack the Glasgow Citizens' and venues in central Scotland; and with *Blood Red Roses*, a play about a militant, a Celtic fighting woman, we toured the Outer Hebrides and the far northern counties, and the Edinburgh Festival Fringe, and Aberdeen and Arbroath and Dundee and St Andrews and Livingstone and Cumbernauld and Stirling Miners Welfare and Craigroyston School – and the men and women and children came in to see it, and most coming out say they really enjoyed it. And many see the stuff they read in their papers and watch on the TV questioned, indeed contradicted: they see a perspective on life that many of them share but are told is not applicable, and are more confident of their own views, their own perspective. And others come out disagreeing, but at least aware that the way of looking at life imposed on the people of Scotland by the Tory consensus of the south-east of England is not the only way of looking at life. And all come out knowing that the working-class movement is not only about strikes, wrecking the economy and wage demands, as they had been led to believe. And that culture is not exclusively in the hands of the children of the rich or the higher-educated: they have culture too, and this theatre is part of their culture, and for that reason they can look outside Bruce Forsyth and *Crossroads* towards their own humanity, and dignity, and creativity, towards, in fact, the immense potential of the human race.